DANIEL BROCKMAN

THE
TALE
OF
CAPITALISM

A Storybook for Non-Economists

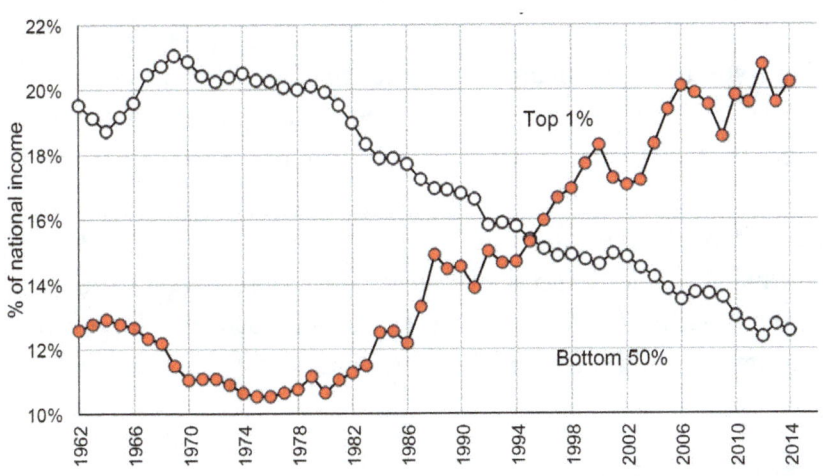

Source: Appendix Table II-B1
"The fall of the bottom 50% mirrors the rise of the top 1%"
Picketty, Saez, Zucman. (2016) *Distributional National Accounts: Methods and Estimates for the United States.*

The Tale of Capitalism: A Storybook for Non-Economists
Copyright 2022 by Daniel Brockman
All rights reserved

This book includes content, such as images, quotations and figures created by others. However, the author intends to use such content made available from the public domain, or with permission, or government sources, or in compliance with fair use doctrines.

Users should seek permission for reuse of lengthy extents of text. Otherwise, the copyright holder accepts users quoting up to two pages, with citation or attribution, without prior permission.

Ordering information:
Quantity sales. Special discounts are available on quantity purchases by schools, associations, and others. For details, contact the publisher via the email below.

Laughing Philosopher Press
info@LaughingPhilosopher.com

Print Edition: 979-8-9864720-2-7
E-Book Edition: 979-8-9864720-3-4

Cover Design: Alberto Besi
Book Design: Lorna Johnson
Photographer: Cheri Dempkowski
Style Editor: Bob Drake

For Linda Cunningham,
who resolutely encouraged me
and read every draft.

*I'm indebted to my friends who gave me the benefits
of their ideas, their comments on prepublication drafts,
their corrections, their criticisms and advice,
their patience and their encouragements.*

I am grateful to Nancy Flack, Dennis Martin, Rock Brockman, Doug Stetson, Don Zirulnik, Richard Leaf, Lorna Johnson, John Brockman, Ken Sherman, Lee Reed, James Reeves, Kazuko Watanabe, Valeta Drake, Maaris Dravnieks, and Tevin Chouinard for their help. I hope I left no one out.

Contents

1   Onto This Stage 1
2   The 90 Percent 9
3   The Buyer of Labor and the Nine Percent 13
4   Workers, GDP, and Economists. 19
5   CEOs, Growth, and Prosperity of Society 23
6   Supercompensation, Income, and The Exchange 27
7   Land and Ricardo 37
8   Managers, Professors, and Engels. 51
9   The Eric Tetralogy: 1: Rents and Monops 65
10   The Eric Tetralogy: 2: The Tea Party 75
11   The Eric Tetralogy: 3: The Firehose Up 85
12   The Eric Tetralogy: 4: Ideas as Monops 93
13   Rand, Marx, and the Downward Trickle. 101
14   Corporations, The Free Market, and the Invisible Hand. 113
15   Capital and the Chairman 123
16   The Old Ones and the 50 Percent 131
17   Growth and Income Disparity 139
18   Encyclopedic Glossary 151

Afterword 205
Images by Chapter. 213
Sources 225
About the Author 243

For much of its history,
economics explained the virtue
and justice of the Aristocracy.

1

Onto This Stage

What determines the level of inequality is above all society's ideological, political, and institutional capacity to justify and structure inequality.

— Thomas Piketty, *Capital and Ideology* (2020)

Sign of the Third Base Tavern (2016)

I went for a long bicycle ride along the Potomac River with my old friend Dr. Stetson and my brother Rock. We stopped at the Third Base Tavern in Williamsport, Maryland, one evening.

While sampling a delicious and unique house-made firewater, we conversationally arrived on the topic of Job Creators, a term widely used as a rough synonym for business owners or entrepreneurs. I said there was no such thing, that while business owners and entrepreneurs existed, they didn't "create jobs." Dr. Stetson said on the contrary that, "obviously," they did. Rock said he proudly had done so. I shook my head. I had no response better than a muttered "It's just not so."

This book is a collection of stories for non-economists, not more and not less. You might remember some parts, more or less, and recount them to friends and children. It does get dense and difficult in places – the Achilles heel of writing about economics. If you hit a tedious spot, don't worry. Just skip on to the next page. If a word presents a puzzle, the Encyclopedic Glossary at the back of the book can help.

I wrote this book for everybody. Of course, that is wishful thinking bordering on hubris, but if you have read this far, then I wrote it for you. Don't let the possibility of not understanding some part of it deter you from reading the parts you do understand.

Before we go too far, let me disclose my political and economic attitudes. I don't generally oppose Capitalism, nor Capitalists, though I disagree with some of them. I'm not a Capitalist in the dispute between Capitalists and anti-Capitalists, nor am I an anti-Capitalist. Nor am I a Communist, Socialist, anti-Communist or anti-Socialist, nor a Liberal, nor a Conservative.

It would be vanity to claim no prejudices. Let me then vainly say I intend no prejudices in matters of politics and economics and history. I feel I don't get net benefit from a biased view. If I have a prejudice, it is that I like democracy.

On with the story…

Capitalism has many variations, though some essential elements occur in all of them. Capitalism occurs in a context that allows individuals to trade what they have for what they want in competitive markets in which some form of cooperation protects a notion of honest trading and a notion of private ownership.

Some early small bands of hunter-gatherers may have shared within their tribe as a happy family might. A gain for one was a gain for all. However, for larger groups and distant tribes, especially since the development of agriculture, we find honest trade, competitive markets, cooperation, and private property in numerous accounts of our collective ancestors. We find them among ancient people (Hughes, 1977; Wilmeth, 1973). The Bible, the book of Genesis mentions trading, buying and selling livestock, food, metals, and people.

Circa 0 A.D., Chinese traded cattle, horses, silk, rice, and other commodities with people from lands to the west (Frankopan, 2015). At the time of Muhammed (ca. 600), Mecca flourished on trade (Bowering, 2015). We find trade, competitive markets, and private property well established in Europe when the first modern corporations appeared around 1600. Up to our enlightened modern era, without question for the last 500 years or more, they seem universal human traits.

Onto this stage strides one to whom circumstances have given a bit more money than she wants to use in the near future. In the marketplace, she trades some money for materials, tools, and workers' labor. With the materials and tools, the workers make something useful which she (or a worker engaged for the purpose) trades in the market for money. The money from the trade reimburses her for the cost of the materials, tools, and labor, plus a little extra. We call the extra the "profit." After reimbursement for expenses, she has the money she started with, plus the profit, which adds up to more total money than before. She can use some of the money for materials, tools, and workers' labor and repeat the process.

We call this person a Capitalist and her repeated activity of trading for additional money we call Capitalism.

Much is right with Capitalism, although there is something wrong with it. Capitalism can reliably distribute bare necessities of life to about 85 or 90 percent of the population, and much more than that to some, which we would consider a splendid accomplishment were it not commonplace. The remaining people, 10 or 15 percent, reliably suffer from their hunger and deprivation.

A few among the population accumulate great wealth, which provides incentives to the Capitalist. Capitalism's opportunities for workers to acquire useful things provides incentives to the workers. The deprivation provides disincentives. The incentives and disincentives encourage trading and vigorous production of useful things.

With the incentives of Capitalism, many people reliably get at least minimum subsistence income, and some get comforts, political power, and even vast riches, while year after year, reliably, Capitalism leaves some persons

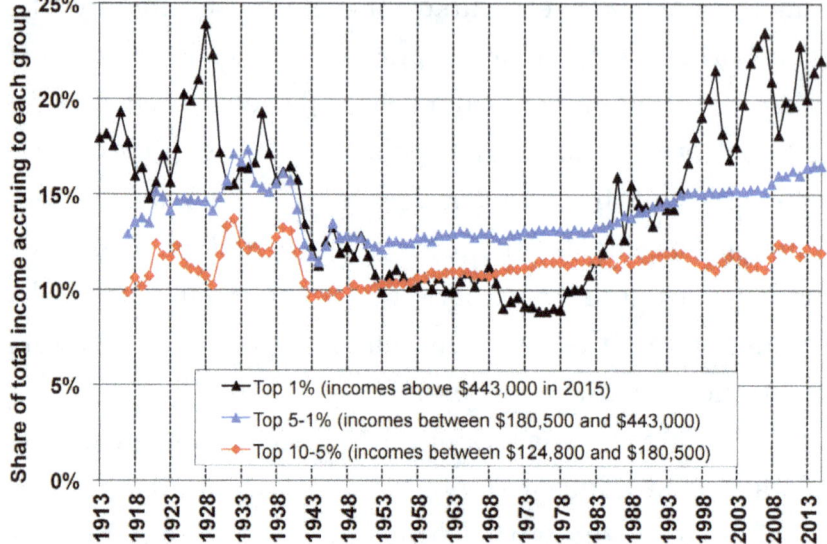

Source: Table A3, cols. P90-95, P99-100. Income is defined as market income including capital gains.
Graph: Emmanuel Saez, "Striking It Richer" (June 30, 2016) eml.berkeley.edu/~saez

deprived and living a scanty existence (Coleman-Jensen, 2016).

I wondered about our economic system predictably allowing a few tens of millions of people to suffer chronic hunger each year. While this isn't criminal since we can't attribute responsibility to any particular persons, do we merely shrug and say that's the way the system works?

In the US, Europe, and other wealthy countries, tens of millions suffer diminished vigor from malnutrition, though few starve to death in these regions. I suppose we might say, "It's the system's fault," which means it's nobody's fault.

In the US, that means if we want it fixed, then it's up to us to fix it. I wondered if there was some less cruel way to incentivize the people. I wondered how we might correct this cruelty of chronic hunger in the system. I had written a few casual blog articles seeking to find and tell the story. I set out to study and report.

Some particular questions drew me. What is Capitalism? Who articulated, discovered, or invented it? What did classic economists say about Capitalism? What creates the great disparity between the poor and the rich? Can we enhance our modern economic system so that it distributes not less than a subsistence minimum to each person, while providing incentives and productivity?

Having a lifelong interest in economics, I have read the works of numerous economists. I read some more, especially of the classic economists, in research for this book. I learned the economists had noticed the benefits and the troubles, which they investigated and debated extensively.

Economic literature and history provide some stories we can readily adapt and summarize here. To render a good story in other cases, I dramatized in Hollywood style. I told some stories straight, embellished others, and made up a few about how it might have happened, always to provide an economic understanding, preferring the simple explanation, approximately right if not precisely correct, that the reader might take along as a memorable story. The identification of the Staffs, as the central actors in production and maintenance of income disparity in our modern enlightened age, and GDP01, GDP09,... are my own characterizations. References allow the interested reader to pursue precise facts.

This book introduces two important words that puzzled readers of the preprint drafts of this book: Monop and Staffs.

A Monop is a Monopoly or Monopsony, depending on context. (A Monopsony is a Firm or person that is the sole buyer in a market with many sellers.) See the Encyclopedic Glossary in the back of the book for summary description. See the chapter "The Eric Tetralogy: 1: Rents and Monops" for detail.

A Staff is an Aristocrat's team of accountants, lawyers, managers, lobbyists, and financial advisors. Many Aristocrats have a Staff to oversee and advise on financial and business concerns. One Aristocrat has a Staff. Two Aristocrats, taken together, have two Staffs. Staffs is the plural of Staff. See the Encyclopedic Glossary.

While I suppose most people will start with the first chapter, some may prefer beginning with a later chapter. No chapter depends too heavily on the previous one. Just have a good time of it.

Daniel Brockman
Gig Harbor, Washington, US
January 26, 2022

2

The 90 Percent

*The Tale of Capitalism, or TOC, is a mythology,
a collection of villains, heroes, morals,
all of which participate from time to time.*

In the United States, 90 percent of the people have about 50% of the income and about 25% of the wealth.

In TOC (Tale of Capitalism), a term can have more than one meaning. "90 Percent" is one of those terms. The 90 Percent consists of the 90% of the Society who have the least wealth or income. Combined with the Ten Percent who have the most wealth or income, they make up all the people in the Society. The 90 Percent includes nearly all of the Workers and the small business owners and all of the poor people.

The 90 Percent don't have 90% of the income in the society, but much less. According to Thomas Piketty (2014, *Capital,* Figure 9.8, p. 324), in the United States, the aggregate income of the 90 Percent declined from a share of about 63% of the aggregate income of Society in 1970 to about 53% in 2010. Emmanuel Saez and Gabriel Zucman found the income share of the 90 Percent fell from 72% of the aggregate income of Society in 1970 to 60% in 2010. According to Saez (2020), the 90 Percent's share of income was about 50% in 2018.

The 90 Percent have much less than 90% of the wealth, too. Per Saez and Zucman, the aggregate wealth of the 90 Percent, as a percentage of the aggregate wealth of Society, declined from about 30% in 1970 to about 25% in 2012, depending on the metric chosen. The World Inequality Database (`wid.world/data`) shows approximately the same values and about 30% in 2018.

Labor is the productive activity of the Workers. Nearly the entire income of the 90 Percent arises from compensation

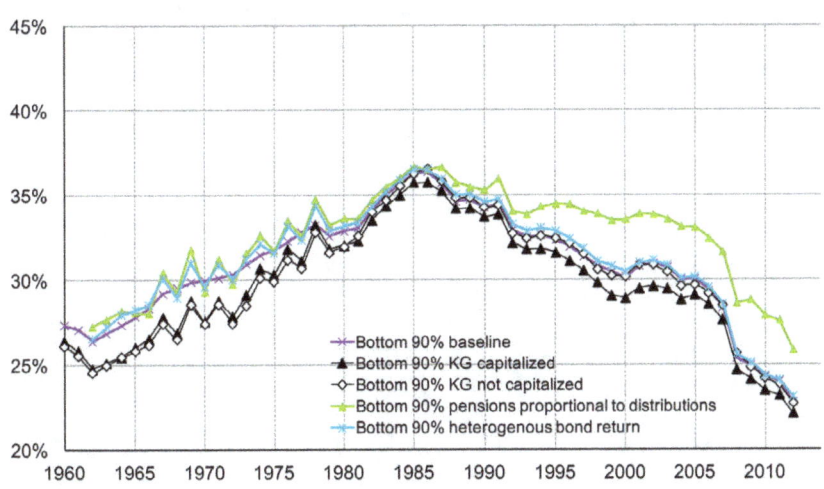

Saez and Zucman (May 2016, The Quarterly Journal of Economics)

for the Labor of Workers. Then we can estimate that at least half of the income of Society is the current value of Labor (more precisely about 70%, as we read on). We will see in the chapter on The Buyer of Labor and the Nine Percent that the Nine Percent account for about 10% of the value of Labor.

Rarely will any two people ever have the same income. Some will have more and some less. A tenth part of the people will enjoy an income exceeding the highest income of the 90 Percent. Still, we contemplate, why would not the value of Labor be 65% or 80% of the income of Society? But that's another story.

In the next chapter, we consider the anatomy of a trade and the value that owners of businesses will exchange for Labor.

3

The Buyer of Labor and the Nine Percent

TOC, the Tale of Capitalism, is not one story, but a saga reflected in many stories.

The fundamental tale of TOC is the Tale of the Trade, which predates the Old Ones. In a trade, at least two people, the "traders," participate. In our glorious era, some traders have instructed robots to perform trades for them. We can regard the trading robot as merely a trader from another tribe. The Fisher and the Dentist is just one of the many variations of the Tale of the Trade.

A trader could give a bucket of fish in exchange for the extraction of a tooth by a dentist. If both parties (the fishing trader and the dentist trader) have a wide range of counterparties (other patients and other dentists) from whom to choose, and if they both participate freely without coercion or deception, then we call it a fair trade.

In a fair trade, both parties benefit. The dentist doesn't have any fish, and she is hungry. The dentist has plenty of tools and experience for extracting teeth, which she can do easily, and a costly certificate hanging on the wall for which she has no use if she doesn't pull a few teeth now and then. The fisher has a sore tooth and more fish than he can eat. When the fisher delivers the bucket of fish and the dentist removes the tooth, they have completed the trade. After the trade, the hungry dentist has fish to eat after giving up nothing but 15 minutes of her time. The fisher, who may have been out in a boat hunting fish for the last three days, has relief from pain after giving up a few fish he couldn't use. Both parties give up something they value relatively less and get something they value relatively more. Both parties benefit.

Clayton Christensen, a Professor, told a story about situations encountered by traders, in our case the fisher, as a person with a "job to be done," a goal to achieve or an obstacle to remove. The story is *The Theory of Jobs To Be Done* (Gerdeman, 2016). The successful search for a product or person contributes to job creation, not to be confused with the Ingenious Innovative Job Creators, but that's another story.

In our advanced era, a trade more often involves money offered in exchange for a good or a service. In these money trades, we call the two traders the Buyer and the Seller. The Buyer gives money to the Seller, and the Seller gives something to the Buyer. For the fisher and the dentist, the fisher first takes the fish he caught to the fish market. The fisher gives the fish to the Buyer of fish who offers him money at the highest price. Now the fisher has money and an aching tooth, and he would be glad to give up some of the money to get relief from the pain. The fisher finds the dentist among the several dentists available. The fisher feels confident, having seen the certificate on the wall. The dentist removes the tooth in a quick procedure. The fisher gives some money to the dentist. The hungry dentist is glad to have some money, with which she can buy food, the certificate on the wall having less value as food. With the money, the dentist goes down to the fish market at the wharf and buys (gives some money for) a fish sandwich.

In the US, the 90 Percent probably includes the fisher. The 90 Percent are the least wealthy 90% of households. In 2018, they had about 30% of the wealth, and they got about 90% of their income from selling their Labor. They received about half the total national income.

We will probably find the dentist among the Nine Percent. In 2015, the income of a household in the Nine Percent was between about $125,000 and about $450,000.

The Nine Percent, together with the Aristocracy (incomes above $450,000 per household in 2015), are the Ten Percent. The Nine Percent get about 30% of national aggregate household incomes; the Aristocracy gets about 20%.

The Ten Percent get about three-quarters of the income growth in the US economy. The Nine Percent get about one-quarter of the total income growth. The Aristocracy gets nearly all the rest.

About 60% of the income of the Nine Percent comes from their Labor and 40% of their income from ownership of capital (stocks, bonds, etc.) and businesses.

The Nine Percent have about 30% of national aggregate capital and business income (Piketty, 2014).

In a fair trade, a Seller has many potential Buyers. The Seller can accept a trade with the Buyer who offers the highest price or terms most favorable to the Seller. A Buyer has many potential Sellers and can agree to a trade with the Seller who offers the lowest price or terms most favorable to the Buyer.

In our enlightened era, Sellers of Labor, the Workers that is, often contend with many other Sellers trading with

USA 2018 Wealth Shares and Pre-Tax Income Shares

Percent	Labor Inc	Capital Inc	Total Inc	Wealth
Aristocracy	6	13	19	35
Nine Percent	16	11	27	36
40 Percent	35	6	41	28
50 Percent	13	0	13	1
Total	70	30	100	100

1. The table summarizes data from several sources. Except as otherwise noted below, the values come from World Inequality Database (wid.world/data, retrieved Nov 2021).
2. The Aristocracy Labor/Capital split from Saez & Zucman (Oct 2020), Figure 27.
3. The 50 Percent have 1% of total wealth. Even if we allow an implausibly high return on capital of 25% annually, their Capital income share of total income rounds to zero. Their Labor income share of Total national income is the remainder, 13%.
4. The Total Labor/Capital income split has remained nearly 70% Labor / 30% Capital for many years, per Picketty, Saez & Zucman (May 2018, gabriel-zucman.eu/files/PSZ2018Slides.pdf).
5. The Labor/Capital income split for the 40 Percent and for the Nine Percent is from updates to appendix data tables for Pikettty, Saez & Zucman (May 2018) and advice provided by Dr. Zucman.

a small number of Buyers (employers). In some industries and locations, the employers have market dominance, which we call "Monopsony" (see the chapter "Eric Tetralogy: 1: Rents and Monops"). In an employers' Monopsony, the Workers have few choices. One could count the potential employers for specialized Labor on one hand and have fingers left over. On the other hand, the employers have many applicants for each job vacancy. The lack of a large number of employers implies few competing Buyers in the Labor market. This lack impairs the fairness of trades available in the market for Labor. The 90 Percent generally work for companies owned by the Ten Percent.

Some of the Professors suggested in their performances that a Free Market is a fair market, naturally correcting itself for imbalances of Buyers and Sellers that may arise from time to time. But that is another story.

Many Professors also performed renditions on the topic of GDP, which we will examine in the next chapter.

4

Workers, GDP, and Economists

The Tale of Capitalism, or TOC, is a mythology, as is the Wild West, portrayed in thousands of movies, radio, and television programs.

Sometimes the Professors created Tales, and sometimes other members of the Society created Tales, but Economists originated most of the Tales. Most people couldn't understand the Economists. The ancient Economists, to whom all turned for their original and enduring wisdom, were called the Old Ones, but that's another story.

In the Tales, Workers were the people who got most of their income from their personal Labor. Sometimes the Economists simply called them Labor. The 90 Percent included almost all Workers. Of the Workers, none were Aristocrats, or if there was an Aristocrat among them, it was most often a scion sent to work in a factory for a summer, or an Aristocrat in disguise, like a monarch (Massie, 1980) or a president of a Federal Reserve Bank (Coleman, 1974) who wanted to learn about the life of a Worker.

The Economists often described GDP (Gross Domestic Product) as the fundamental measure of social wellbeing. GDP in the United States was mainly National Income plus depreciation of Capital, which resembled an accountant's concept of cash flow. Depreciation of Capital was about one-sixth of GDP, a relatively stable and predictable amount compared with National Income. A few relatively minor adjustments wrapped up the calculation. So, GDP differed little from National Income. Significant changes in the GDP level were almost always the underlying significant change in National Income.

The Professors studied the Economists carefully and composed performances about the Tales. Many people could understand the performances. The people told stories of

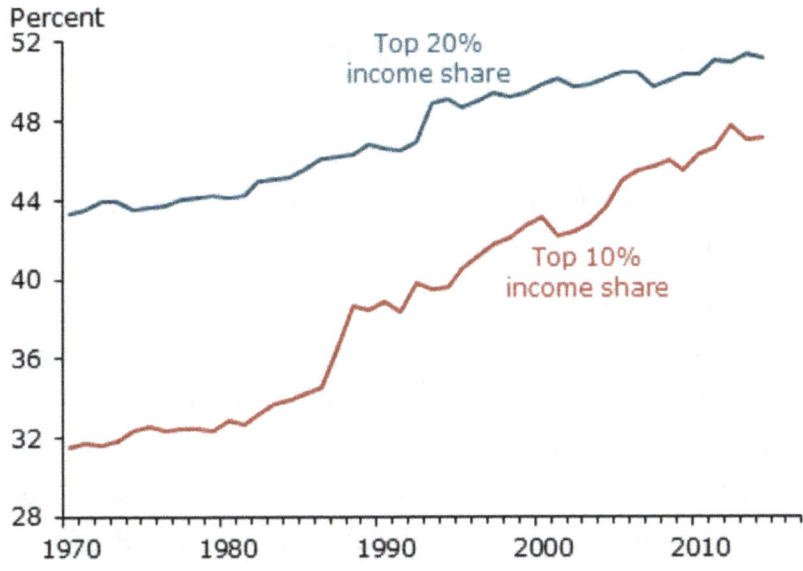

Source: Census Bureau (Table H-2), World Top Incomes database
Graph: Lansing and Markiewicz, "Consequences of Rising Income Inequality" (2016)

some of the more memorable performances to their friends, who in turn told their friends. That was how most people learned of the Tales. *Growth of GDP* was perhaps the Professors' favorite performance topic. During the time of the great wars, and ever since, these performances drew large attentive audiences who learned that the growth of GDP was good for everyone.

For a few years following the great wars of the 20th century, many Economists believed that Aristocrats, the Nine Percent and the 90 Percent shared, more or less evenly, the growth of GDP. But in the 21st century, GDP01 (the Aristocrats' share of GDP), GDP09 (the share collected by the Nine Percent), and GDP90 (everyone else's share), grew at different rates.

From 1977 to 2007, growth of GDP10 (= GDP01 + GDP09) was three-fourths of the growth of GDP. Even when GDP grew nicely, GDP90 grew only a little from year to year. At the same time, GDP09 grew fast, and GDP01 grew even faster. GDP growth wasn't distributed evenly at all. The Ten Percent got most of the GDP growth.

In legend and rumor, the Workers knew their incomes didn't grow much. They didn't understand GDP numbers. They knew GDP growth was a good thing because they heard the people on television report the numbers as good things. The people on television also interviewed Professors sometimes, and the Professors said GDP growth was a good thing. The Workers had faith that disciplined work and a little bit of luck would make them as rich as Aristocrats.

They would have known had they remembered the performances heard by some of their grandfathers 100 years earlier. The Old Ones had written some Tales that inspired Workers, and Professors rendered these Tales as performances. But that's another story.

5

CEOs, Growth, and Prosperity of Society

A deep motif of TOC, the Tale of Capitalism, is that a wealthy Aristocrat getting richer benefits Workers and Society.

Once upon a time, growth measured prosperity in the Society. *Growth of GDP,* the kind of growth they had in mind, was perhaps the Professors' favorite topic in their repertoire. In *Growth of GDP,* performed often, prosperity followed growth. Some listeners envisioned enlarging the Aristocrats' wealth and letting the Downward Trickle distribute the prosperity to the 99 Percent, but that is another story.

Society, of course, was all the people (the Aristocrats, the Nine Percent, and the 90 Percent). To find, gather, produce and distribute stuff in large proportions, Society organized itself into groups called Firms.

A CEO (Chief Executive Officer), sometimes called the President, was the Manager who outranked all other Managers in a Firm. The CEO could tell any of the Workers and any of the other Managers what to do. By hiring appropriate Managers and Workers, the CEO worked to improve the Shareholders' part of GDP10, and incidentally the CEO's part due to the potential conflict of interest (see the Encyclopedic Glossary).

CEOs had varied origins. Some founded the Firm, the usual case with the smaller Firms. Many were Managers who had pleased the previous CEO, often by their performance at other Firms. Sometimes, the CEO was a close relative of the previous CEO. For older or larger Firms, especially those in which the previous CEO was Aristocratic, the CEO was an Aristocrat from birth. Sometimes a Board selected as CEO a Worker who had become a Manager and who had shown talent.

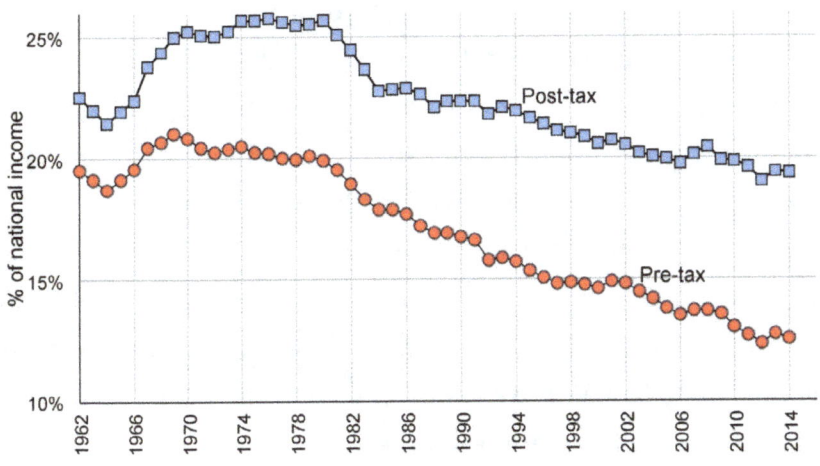

United States income shares. Graph: Saez, Piketty, and Zucman (Dec 2016)

GDP50 shrank during the 50 years ended 2014

The Staffs of the Aristocrats usually didn't include the CEOs, but not uncommonly a member of a Staff was chosen as CEO. Sometimes a Staffer became a CEO when an Aristocrat wanted a person of demonstrated talent, instead of a son or niece or paramour of presumed talent, to manage a Firm, reminiscent of the Ottomans (Bowering et al, 2013).

The Economist Piketty presented pictures showing prosperity wasn't evenly distributed among the Society. GDP01 (which included depreciation from the Ten Percent's ownership of large companies) wasn't much smaller than GDP90. Piketty's graphs showed GDP50 grew ever more slowly as the years had passed and then shrank. GDP90 slowed to nearly no growth at all. GDP10 grew nicely, though ever more slowly. In later years, overall GDP growth sometimes outpaced GDP10. GDP01 grew rapidly over the years, though with variability.

Responding to the conflict between Piketty's pictures and their favorite topic, some Professors modified the traditional rendition of *Growth of GDP* describing how even though Society's income distribution allocated much growth to the Ten Percent, that was necessary for the 90 Percent to experience any growth. But most continued to perform the classic version, which members of Governments understood well, owing to their frequent discussions with the Staffs, who the Professors had educated.

The Economists held their colleague Saez in high regard in part for the extensive data studies, graphics and mathematics that he brought to his work. Saez, a frequent collaborator with Piketty, described how the Supercompensation that the Boards paid the CEOs in the period following the great wars grew to about 40% of the aggregate incomes of the Aristocracy. But that's another story.

6

Supercompensation, Income, and The Exchange

*Causes of Civil War are also, that the Wealth
of the Nation is in too few mens hands,
and that no certain means are provided
to keep all men from a necessity
either to beg, or steal, or be Souldiers.*

– William Petty 1623-1687

Once upon a time, a small, small number of people in the Society received a large, large amount of pay for their work. So large an amount did this small number of people receive that it accounted for a significant part of the National Income.

Sculpture: Brenda Putnam. (1950). *Solon.*

In those days, there was a young man who received a good education and became an employee receiving an annual pay of $55,000. His colleagues liked him and regarded him highly. He reliably exceeded short-term goals while remaining consistent with the long-term plan. He worked with versatility and insight. He was diligent, clever, persistent, adaptable, creative, and quite productive. He worked with devotion to customers, colleagues, Society, and the Shareholders. He never wasted the Firm's resources, though he didn't shirk from taking a calculated business risk. His work advanced long-term strategic growth and drove strong results. He advised junior colleagues on their career development. He embraced change, improved product quality, innovated new processes and products, spoke truth to power, focused on the customer, and led his colleagues in grasping new challenges. His Managers observed his consistently superior performance. Each and every year, for his meritorious performance, he received an increase of 10% in his rate of pay plus compensation for inflation, a reward for good work, and an implied incentive to perform well in the future. After 30 years of superior performance, no longer young, with promotions to new responsibilities and the 10% increase each year, he received annual pay of nearly $1 million.

The CEO of the same Firm received Supercompensation of about $18 million per year.

We'll return to the excellent worker and the CEO, but first, what is this thing called National Income? And for that matter, how do we define Income?

The Economists calculated National Income as GDP minus depreciation of capital plus or minus some relatively minor adjustments, mostly for transactions with foreign parties.

The Aristocracy got about 20%, or $3 trillion in the US, of National Income. Of that, about two-thirds was Capital Income, and the remaining one-third, or about $1 trillion, was Labor Income for the Aristocracy.

United States 2016	$ Trillions
GDP (Gross Domestic Product)	19
Less: Depreciation	– 3
Equals: National Income	16

Source: BEA.gov, Table 1.7.5

Customarily, in those days, many people received money, called "pay," in exchange for the Labor of some members of their household. The people could exchange the money for the necessities of life and a degree of personal indulgence. Some of the people saved a part of their pay for future use. From about a third to a half of the people received subsistence pay or less, so urgent present needs seldom left money for saving and future use.

A different arrangement called "slavery" prevailed in earlier times, but most of the people knew of slavery from legends. Slavery enabled some people to use threats of bodily harm to force Labor from Workers called "slaves," who were bought and sold like livestock. If slaves received pay in extraordinary situations, they rarely got much of it, but that is a different story.

Another arrangement, sometimes called "debt slavery," wasn't uncommon in earlier times, but most of the people had forgotten it. Even though Solon of Athens had prohibited some forms of debt slavery, the arrangement persisted elsewhere even 2,500 years later, even during the time of the great wars. In one form, an employer paid Workers money insufficient for bare subsistence and lent additional money to the Workers for rent in housing the employer owned and for food from a store the employer owned. With loan payments deducted from their pay, Workers borrowed even more, and so remained under perpetual obligation to the employer. But that too is a different story.

However, the Workers, in this (longish) story of Supercompensation, Income and The Exchange, didn't live in the time of slavery. For the most part, and like nearly all of the 99 Percent, the Workers were employees of Firms. For a few, around 9/10ths of their Income came from exchanging their Labor for money. For most of the Workers, though, all their income came from Labor. If you didn't have Capital Income, then you had to give Labor to get Income.

The norms of Society (with some exceptions in this immense population, of course) held to the belief that without the principle of Labor for Income, civilization would be lost. Maybe it didn't have to be that way, but that's how it was.

Households had median annual income of about $55,000. Many Workers got pay of about that much, which was nearly all of their income. A Worker with five times that pay was quite well paid and characteristic of the upper reaches of the 99 Percent and approaching that of the less wealthy Aristocrats.

For the average Aristocrat, Income came mostly from the ownership of Firms and the lending of money, which the Economists called Capital Income, and about one-third to one-half from Labor Income. Supercompensation, a form of Labor Income, became a more important component of Aristocratic Income following the great wars.

But all that's a regression into old rumors and legends. Let's get back to story of the excellent Worker who merited a pay increase of 10% per year plus inflation from the Firm that employed him, and the Firm's CEO who received Supercompensation.

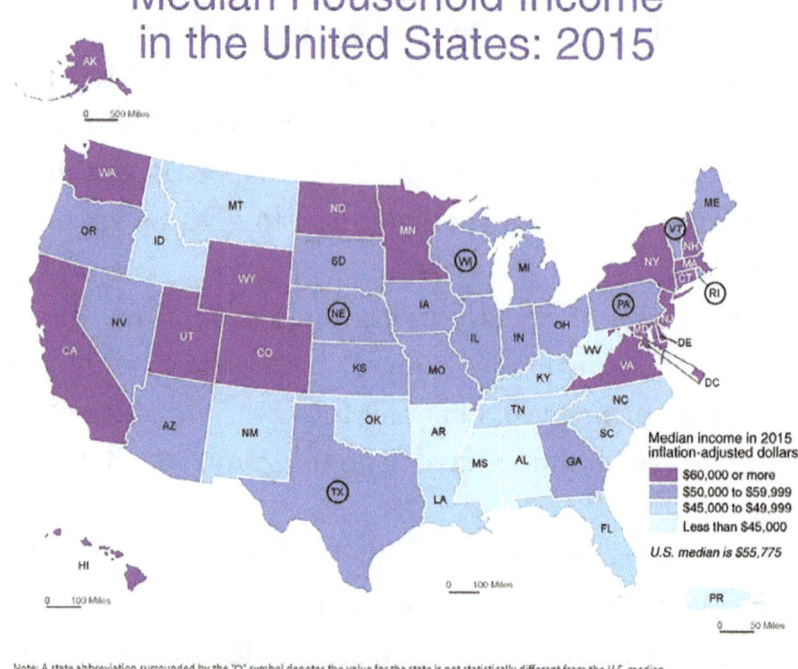

The Firm's shares were traded at the Exchange, a big granite building where representatives of people who wanted to own part of the Firm would buy shares from representatives of Shareholders of the Firm who wanted to sell some of their shares.

The word "Exchange" also referred to the association of members, like a club, that met every day at the big granite building. The members never ran on the floor of the Exchange. The members were the representatives who bought and sold shares of various Firms. They would buy or sell shares for you if you paid them their fee. Their revenues came from their fees and from buying shares for a few pennies less than the price for which they immediately sold them. They bore the costs of trading paperwork and of the Exchange membership, which they had bought from someone else. Like all other businesses, the Incomes of the members were their revenues less their costs.

The Exchange's members had rules limiting the character of the shares they traded. They had created many of these rules at the insistence of Government, which usually allowed the members to pretend the rules were voluntary. The historical reason for this custom of pretending the rules were voluntary was lost even to the Old Ones, most of whom had been dead a long time. The Society kept the custom for the same reason they placed the forks on the left sides of their plates.

One set of Exchange rules required Firms with shares traded on the Exchange to make public the amounts paid to the most highly paid employees every year with explanations for why they paid that much. The most highly paid employee was usually, but not always, the CEO.

Usually, but not always, the second most highly paid employee received a much smaller amount of money than the CEO, though often the second most highly paid employee received Supercompensation, too.

There was no legal limit to the number of employees who could receive Supercompensation, but few Firms paid it to more than five of their employees.

Examples of Supercompensation in 2016

ticker	name	business	most highly paid emp $m	mkt cap $b	price 170331	Last checked
GOOGL	Alphabet	online, cloud iaas top 10, advertising, AI	100.6	300.5	847.80	170319
REGN	Regeneron	Pharma	47.5	38.7	387.51	170323
ORCL	Oracle	Cloud, Databases	41.5	184.3	44.61	170323
IBM	IBM	AI, computing, cloud	32.7	164.9	174.14	170323
JNJ	Johnson & Johnson	Healthcare products	26.9	341.3	124.55	170323
ALXN	Alexion Pharma	Pharma for genetic illnesses	24.9	26.8	121.24	170326
OMC	Omnicom	advertising, CRM, PR	23.6	19.8	86.21	170326
AAPL	Apple	phones	22.9	734.5	143.66	170319
TSLA	Tesla	Electric Car, Mars, Solar Power	20.9	42.3	278.30	170319
BA	Boeing	Aircraft	20.9	106.9	176.86	170326

Chart: Daniel Brockman

To explain why they paid these large amounts of Supercompensation, the Board of the Firm appointed a Committee of Compensation of three of its members, usually two CEOs and one Executive from other Firms. First, the Committee hired a consultancy, a kind of business that provided Staff on demand. The consultancy researched the matter carefully. After several months, the consultancy provided two or three dozen pages of intensely boring prose for inclusion, with approval of the Committee of Compensation, in the Notice to Shareholders of Annual Meeting and Proxy Statement.

With the consultancy's text, the Proxy Statement explained how the CEO upheld the Firm's devotion to customers, employees, Society and the Shareholders. It explained how the CEO exceeded short-term goals while remaining consistent with the long-term plan (except for a pesky little legal problem), advanced long-term strategic growth drivers, drove strong results in all parts of the Firm, and got general concurrence from the Shareholders on pay in the previous year.

The Proxy Statement also gave details on the competition with other Firms to pay highly for CEO talent, the extensive industry experience of the CEO, levels of pay (without giving specific numbers) at other Firms of similar size and complexity, various methods of deciding appropriate pay devised by the consultancy and Staff, executive benefits and an abundance of other detail.

The Shareholders who paid any attention ignored most of the detail, looked quickly at the total in the Summary Compensation Table part of the Proxy Statement, then voted yes. And that's why the CEO got Supercompensation.

The Economist Thomas Piketty (2014, ch.14) said the CEOs exercised "bargaining power" to extract the higher rates of pay. The Economists Piketty, Emmanuel Saez, and Stefanie Stantcheva (2014, p.231) attributed an aggressive bargaining response to reduced top marginal income taxation as a possible cause of Supercompensation. They said on the other hand that the CEOs might have been paid for luck. On yet another hand, they said that CEOs might indeed merit their Supercompensation.

The Economist Dean Baker said that the CEOs collected Rents (2016, p.18), unless the value the Firm received was about equal to the money paid to the CEO. CEOs receiving Supercompensation, he wrote, got money that could only have been taken from funds that the Firm otherwise would have paid to other employees or to Shareholders or as reductions in prices for customers.

"Rents" was a word Economists liked to use to describe money a person could get simply because she or he was in a circumstance to demand it. They picked it up from the writings of David Ricardo, one of the Old Ones. Ricardo described how the value of older agricultural land increased when farmers cultivated new lands nearby. But that is another story.

Part of the Professors' topic, *Market Value,* described how the CEOs' Supercompensation fully reflected the CEOs' value because it was tempered by the competition of many buyers and sellers. Customarily, when a CEO recognized the wisdom of the Professors, as often happened, the CEO would endow a chair in Economics at a university.

Some Workers wondered why the excellent employee of 30 years topped out at $1 million per year when the CEO got $18 million per year. But most Workers knew the Professors' *Market Value* topic had the right idea, more or less. They taught their children that good children, with hard work, would have Supercompensation when they grew up.

7

Land and Ricardo

*Often, the Staffs of the Aristocrats,
and sometimes the Aristocrats themselves,
would mention the motifs
of the Tale of Capitalism.*

David Ricardo

Once upon a time, the Old One David Ricardo (1772-1823) composed some of the earliest Tales, which evolved with retellings to become parts of modern economics. Among others, these include LTV (the Labor Theory of Value), a correction to the Theory of Rents advanced by Adam Smith, another Old One, and another theory called the Principle of Comparative Advantage. The Professors included these Tales in their repertoires long after the great wars. In this chapter, we get better acquainted with Ricardo, dash through Rents on Land, then dash through the Comparative Advantage and wind up contemplating some omissions.

Ricardo was a trader. He looked for differences in the values of securities (shares, bonds and financial contracts) that had the same price, and differences in the prices for securities that had the same value. Taking advantage of these differences, he became wealthy trading on the Exchange. He ran for office and became a member of the British Parliament in 1818.

Since he was an Old One, we think of Ricardo as wise, though charmingly antique in his Tales. Charm suggests that we understand the Tales clearly, but we don't. If we were Professors, our incomes would depend partly on our understanding the Old Ones, and even the cleverer of us might struggle with Ricardo.

Ricardo left unexplained gaps in his Tales, as though a carpenter had overlooked erecting a wall of a house, or a portrait painter omitted a subject's eyeball. We persist in seeking understanding, though complexity and missing parts impair our progress.

Like all Old Ones, Ricardo was an Economist. According to Dr. Carlos, one of my own Professors, the House of Commons hired Ricardo to lecture them on Economics. Ricardo's Tales often twist into lists of cases, for example, plots of Land put under cultivation as Farms No. 1, No. 2, and No. 3 of equal area, producing respectively 180 quarters, 150 quarters, and 120 quarters of corn, requiring Labor contributions of 10 Workers each, with equal Capital contributions, and with corn selling for 6 shillings per quarter.

Our heads fill to capacity with the tangle of numbers. Even so, at this point in his Tale, he changes something in the list. Then he rolls through the entire list again tracing out the numbers that changed and the numbers that didn't change. We understand that the change matters, and we understand he portrays it to show us the change. We get kaleidoscopic feelings. We wonder if we've witnessed a magician's sleight-of-hand illusion.

So, when reading the following summaries of some of Ricardo's Tales, if the paragraph gets too dense, many others have felt that way. If you like, just skip to the next picture or table or paragraph or chapter.

Despite these concerns, we can appreciate much of Ricardo's work with understanding.

Ricardo's Tale of the Theory of Rents, as he wrote it, refers to corn measured in quarters and sold for shillings. After the great wars, hardly anyone in the Society measured quantities of corn in quarters (a quarter is a grain measure equal to 8 bushels). Most people didn't know what a quarter was, except maybe $0.25, which made no sense in understanding Ricardo.

Some Professors rumored that Ricardo's corn wasn't like popcorn, or grits, or a big yellow ear, or the corn in taco chips, but rather something like wheat.

Most people living in the modern Society know a shilling as an archaic unit of currency that nobody uses any more, due to the difficulty to explain how to count shillings.

British shilling.

Ricardo's Theory of Rents was perhaps his most powerful Tale. Ricardo described Rents as income from Land. And Land was one of the three factors of production: Labor, Land and Capital. Adam Smith (1776, Bk. I, ch. XI) said Rents are money a person can get while hardly doing a lick of work. Ricardo said the Rent getter has something the nearest competitor can't offer.

We will summarize the explanation of Rents, but as elsewhere in TOC (the Tale of Capitalism), if the tangle of numbers becomes a blur, just skip to the song in italics.

Ricardo said that when the farmer establishes Farm

No. 1, there aren't any other farms around. The Land of this first farm, like all the other Land around, hasn't any previous use, nor any other current use. The farmer can as easily plow the adjacent plot of Land not under another landlord's control, so the Land of Farm No. 1 has no value until farmed. The landlord lets the farmer cultivate the unused Land for a modest fraction of the crop, just a ceremonial payment to seal the contract, because otherwise the landlord would get nothing, and if the farmer worked the land without a payment for many years, the landlord might forfeit his ownership under common law.

The farmer chooses this Land for Farm No. 1 because it has the best soil and drainage and other helpful attributes. The farmer's employees work the Land for all it can produce, which is 180 quarters of corn in that year, which fetches 900 shillings (5 shillings per quarter) at the market. With the 900 shillings, the farmer pays the wages of the employees and the costs of fencing, plows, a wagon to take the quarters of corn to market, a shilling for the Land contract, and return on Capital, a.k.a. profit, which is a few shillings for his own pocket.

After a few years of corn production, the well-fed population grows more numerous and there are offers to buy more corn. A farmer cultivates Farm No. 2 to meet the demand. Now No. 1 is on the best land, and No. 2 is less well endowed (otherwise No. 2 would have been chosen for cultivation first). No. 2 produces only 150 quarters with the same amount of Labor. 150 quarters at 5 shillings is 750 shillings from Farm No. 2. Plus, No. 1 still produces

180 quarters, also at 5 shillings for 900 shillings. The landlord of Farm No. 1 now demands the difference, 150 shillings (= 900 - 750) as Rent on No. 1, the prime Land. No. 2 produces no Rent, because that Land is otherwise unused and any Rent would wipe out the return on Capital. The farmer of Farm No. 1 may complain, since the landlord's cut will reduce the farmer's profits. The farmer may persuade the Labor to take a lower wage, but then might lose the experienced Workers to Farm No. 2. The farmer might merely walk away, unable to get a satisfying return on Capital. The farmer perhaps can get 6 shillings a quarter at the market, and this might work out for the current season, but the Workers would demand more pay so they could buy food for their families at the new higher price, or the landlord might demand yet more Rent owing to the difference of 180 shillings (= 1080 − 900) between the returns from No. 1 and No. 2. At a higher market price, some other farmer may cultivate Farm No. 3 and produce 120 quarters per season, which would cause nonzero Rent on Farm No. 2. The farmer can perhaps persuade the landlord to accept 100 shillings for Rent on No. 1 instead of 150. Some adjustment will occur.

The population expands further, demanding more corn. A farmer tells a merchant that with the cost of Labor and Capital such as they are, the farmer can't plow Farm No. 3 profitably at 5 shillings per quarter, because the price wouldn't pay the Workers and the return on Capital. The merchant, who expects to sell corn to the population, offers 6 shillings per quarter. The farmer agrees, hires some

Workers and cultivates No. 3. At harvest, No. 1 produces 1080 shillings (= 6 shillings x 180 quarters), No. 2 produces 900 shillings (= 6 x 150), and No. 3 produces 720 shillings (= 6 x 120).

The landlords demand from the farmers a Rent of 540 shillings, which is 360 shillings (= 1080 - 720) for No. 1, 180 shillings (= 900 - 720) for No. 2 and nothing for No. 3.

When the Professors rendered Ricardo's Tale of Rents as a drinking song, they roared out this chorus:

> *Higher rent causes higher price,*
> *Said Adam Smith,*
> *But in this he erred-oh.*
> *Higher price causes higher rent,*
> *Correctly saw Ricard-oh.*

With apologies to the Old One, and to economize your time, we shall put Ricardo's Labor Theory of Value aside, for that's another story.

Ricardo's most penetrating insight comes down to us, gleaming like a brilliant star. We know it as the "Principle of Comparative Advantage." In Chapter 7 of *Principles* (1821), "On Foreign Trade," in a Tale tricky to relate and slippery in the understanding, Ricardo identified a country's Comparative Advantage, that which it does best, as the country's best choice for export. As in many of his Tales, Ricardo tangles the understanding by weaving in an additional plot line, this one concerning the mechanics of trade finance. And as in all his Tales, the source of value is the Labor required to produce the value.

Again, we summarize a tangle of numbers. And again, if it gets incomprehensible, then skip the math.

In the Tale of Comparative Advantage, there are two countries, England and Portugal. England can produce 1,000 bolts of cloth with the Labor of 100 Workers in one year. Or England can produce 1,000 bottles of wine with the Labor of 150 Workers in one year. England can more easily produce a bolt of cloth, which requires less work, than a bottle of wine.

If England produces 20 fewer bottles of wine, that's 2% of production, and 2% fewer of the 150 Workers, or 3 Workers, will be idled from wine production. Those 3 Workers might go to work at the textile mill. The 100 textile Workers will become 103, a 3% increase, and they will produce 3% more cloth, which is 30 bolts more. So 3 workers can produce 30 bolts of cloth or 20 bottles of wine.

In this sense, 3 bolts of cloth are worth 2 bottles of wine. For every bottle of wine, England gives up 1.50 (= 3/2 = 150/100) bolts of cloth. Wine takes more work than cloth, so we say that England has a Comparative Advantage in producing cloth.

Portugal, owing to different circumstances, produces 1,000 bottles of wine with the Labor of only 80 Workers in one year, and 90 Workers can produce 1,000 bolts of cloth in a year. Portugal more easily produces wine than cloth. Portugal can export wine in exchange for cloth, even though they could produce the cloth locally with less

Making Cloth. Photo by Louis Hine ca. 1937

Labor than England could produce cloth. For every bottle of wine, Portugal gives up 0.89 = (80/90) bolts of cloth. Portugal has a comparative advantage in producing wine.

Suppose Portugal shifts 16 Workers out of cloth production and into wine, then Portugal can produce and export 200 bottles to England. Those 200 bottles trade for 300 bolts of cloth in England to take back to Portugal. Portugal now has 1,000 bottles of wine — 1,200 bottles produced by 96 Workers, less 200 bottles exported to England — and 1,122 bolts of cloth, 822 produced locally by 74 Workers (= 1,000 * (90 - 16)/90), plus 300 from England.

And England shifts 30 Workers out of wine production to put 130 Workers to producing 1,300 bolts of cloth. England gives 300 bolts of cloth to Portugal and gets 200 bottles of wine. England now has 1,000 bolts of cloth produced by 130 Workers, and 1,100 bottles of wine, 800 produced locally by 120 Workers (= 1,000 * (150 - 30)/150), plus 300 from Portugal.

	Without Trade	**With Trade**
England	1,000 wine & 1,000 cloth	1,100 wine & 1,000 cloth
Portugal	1,000 wine & 1,000 cloth	1,000 wine & 1,122 cloth

Comparative Advantage

Both England and Portugal have more stuff by concentrating on their comparative advantages than they would have had by producing everything locally. Ricardo reveals the surprising and profound insight of the Principle of Comparative Advantage: Portugal benefits from trading with England even though Portugal makes both wine and cloth better than England makes either wine or cloth.

Ricardo mentions that, in theory, capitalists and consumers will prefer for Labor to migrate to Portugal, there to make both wine and cloth. The returns to Capital are higher and the cost of product lower. In practice, both Capital and Labor encounter constraints in migrating among countries.

But Ricardo left some things out. In *Principles,* an hour of Labor has the same value, whether spent making wine or cloth. In Chapter 5, "On Wages," Ricardo clearly states the natural price of Labor, the wage, will never long remain much more nor less than the minimum subsistence, just enough to stay alive long enough to return to work next week. If the wage rises unusually high, as sometimes it will, then Workers will prosper, and their numbers will increase.

When the number of Workers increases beyond the demand for Labor, then the wage falls. When it falls even below the level of subsistence minimum, as sometimes it will, then privation will reduce the number of Workers, until demand exceeds the supply of Labor. So, the ability of Workers to buy food and goods changes little from the minimum subsistence.

We see that England has more wine when England trades with Portugal, and Portugal has more cloth. The Workers receive approximately the same wage, enough to survive, and not enough to buy more wine and cloth. Though the country has more wine and cloth, an individual Worker has no more than she had before. Ricardo's Tale doesn't say who gets the additional wine and cloth.

Another omission from Ricardo's Tale concerns the fates of Portuguese cloth Workers who can't find a vineyard to hire them because they haven't sufficient experience at winemaking. The cloth mill has curtailed operations and demands less Labor. The Workers' total wages from making cloth no longer suffice to maintain their families and they face privation. Ricardo doesn't tell us in any detail what becomes of the Workers. He says the privation reduces the supply of Labor.

Ricardo, the wise Old One left out these parts. We can't fault him for all he didn't do, for which of us has not left something undone? Euclid didn't describe gravity, and Newton didn't discover electrons. Euclid and Newton described some profound and enduring principles, and so did Ricardo.

Ricardo lived in an ancient age when Land and Labor had great importance in production and distribution of goods and services in the Society. Dr. Leigh Shaw-Taylor (2010) and his colleagues at the Cambridge Group for the History of Population and Social Structure estimated the occupational distribution of England and Wales in 1817 from baptismal records of the occupations of fathers, militia records and other sources.

About 35% of the working population worked in agriculture, cultivating the Land. Another 40% were in "secondary" occupations, manufacturing goods from agricultural and mining products, including large numbers employed in textiles, construction, footwear, clothing, and food. The remainder were "tertiary" roles such as merchants, dealers, government, and transportation.

Incidentally, the statistical tables show 1.31% of occupations were "Distinguished, titled, gentleman," and 0.03% were "Owners, possessors of capital." Almost everyone in those times had some understanding of agricultural Land, Labor, and Capital.

Killington Parish, UK Baptism Register (1820)

In the modern Society, after the great wars, agriculture had diminished in importance. The United States Bureau of the Census reported (Caruso, 2015) that for 2012, agriculture employed 161,000 Americans, less than 0.2% of all employed persons. Most people knew almost nothing about farming and Land Rents.

In the modern Society, Capital had risen in importance, and sophisticated machines began to displace Workers.

In the modern Society, IP (Intellectual Property) and market domination produced Rents similar to Rents on Land described by David Ricardo. Some economists (Baker, 2016; Piketty, Saez & Stantcheva, 2014) said that CEOs sought Rents as Supercompensation, but that is another story.

Some Workers in the modern Society worried that trade with foreigners would displace them from their source of wages. They became suspicious of the Professors who appeared on television. They became suspicious of theories. Good children who listened to their parents learned some version of Snepscheut's principle:

> *In theory, there is no difference between theory and practice, but in practice, there is.*
>
> *– attributed to Jan L. A. van de Snepscheut*

8

Managers, Professors, and Engels

*Management matters a lot,
but it doesn't matter as much as you think
(especially if you are management).*

– Jason Zweig, 2021

Friedrich Engels 1820-1895

Once upon a time, a German boy dropped out of high school. His father sent the boy to Bremen to take a job that we of modern times would call an intern office clerk. He read the philosopher Hegel, a lecturer in German universities, in his spare time. He also wrote controversial newspaper articles. His mother begged him to stop writing such scandalous ideas.

His name was Friedrich Engels, the "forgotten" Old One. At 21, he joined the army, which ordered him to Berlin. Thus began his adventure. His writings would shake the world. The aftershocks continue even in our modern times.

Engels attended university classes but never got a degree. He hung out with a group called the "Young Hegelians." He continued to write controversial articles for newspapers.

Before long, Engels went to Manchester in Lancashire, England, to work with his father's partner in the Manchester office of the family business, a thread factory in that city. At the time, Manchester and the surrounding Lancashire County were the world's manufacturing center.

Manchester throbbed with innovative, advanced technologies, using steam and water to power spindles and looms for manufacturing textiles. The city hosted an array of other industries as well. It was full of factories, each employing many workers, a way of working made possible by powered machinery. Manchester was a boom town.

Engels took interest in the lives and working conditions of the factory Workers. He went down from

Sir Richard Arkwright, one of Lancashire's early capitalists.

the company office to get to know them. He visited them on the job. He wandered the streets at all hours, ate and drank with the workers, and learned what he could of their ways. He took copious notes. To his German editor, he sent several articles that he subsequently collected into the book *The Condition of the Working Class in England* (1845), both a detailed economic history and a polemic.

Engels wrote *Condition* in the style that the times favored. You may recognize this style from your reading his contemporary Charles Dickens. Long strings of words form sentences that often cascade over two or three pages.

Engels documented the poverty in which many Lancashire Workers died from starvation and disease.

The Workers typically shared a bed of rags with six or eight family members and companions in one of several small rooms in a leaky house without furniture.

He saw children, women and men working 70 or 80 hours per week for wages of pennies. He read reports of doctors, police, and government agencies describing the illnesses of Workers living in squalor.

In the factories, strained working postures and dangerous equipment injured Workers. Bad light and detailed work blinded makers of lace and fine threads. If they survived, infirmities often disabled them for work. An old person among them lived to 40 or 50 years of age.

The Workers, or "proletarians," in the textile factories of Manchester had no, or very little, property from which to get income. Engels included the petite bourgeoisie, the people who owned small shops selling modest goods, among the proletarians. Their lack of property distinguished them from the bourgeoisie, the capitalists who owned property, among whom he included the nobility. To sustain their lives, the proletarians had only their Labor. For most of them, the wages of Labor sufficed to sustain their lives for only the next few days.

Ricardo (1841, ch.5) said the value of Labor seldom varied for long from the cost of the subsistence minimum. The capitalist collected the full price of the product, less the Rent paid for the Land, the costs of materials and tools, and the wages paid to Labor. The capitalist's profit captured the value of changes in the price of product. The Rent on Land depended on its usefulness relative to other

Samuel Compton's Spinning Mule (circa 1779), image by Pezzab

tracts of Land. The wages of Labor tended toward the value of necessities to sustain the Workers' human lives. The value of necessities seldom changed much. Wages and Rent didn't vary with the price of the product. If a high product price or lower cost of production occurred, neither Rent nor wages would increase, but the additional value would increase Capital.

Technical innovation enabled new methods that could reduce the cost of production because they could produce much more product with the same quantity of Labor, or the same quantity of product with less Labor. The lower cost of production enabled a lower price for the product, even while enabling the capitalist to add additional value to Capital.

People who wove cloth by hand in their cottages fell on bad times. They couldn't sell their product at the low prices of goods made by machines. The cottage weavers moved to Lancashire to find work in the factories.

The owners of property, the "bourgeoisie" or "middle class," as Engels called them, began receiving orders for manufactured goods from distant markets, colonies, and other countries where buyers couldn't get similar goods so cheaply from local sources.

To meet demand, the owners would activate idle factory capacity, hiring Labor from the "unemployed reserve" to operate the machines. As orders continued, owners invested Capital to buy the latest versions of automated spinning machines and hired more Labor from the unemployed reserve.

Orders grew in size and number. Commerce boomed. Unemployed Workers became scarce during short periods of the boom. To fill the last vacancies in the factory, the bourgeois owner offered more pay for short periods.

The Workers liked the housing and improved diet that the higher wages made available. The better pay brought more Workers to the factories. The factory owner called for additional production in anticipation of future orders, which continued to arrive for a few years. Bourgeois neighbors, encouraged by the example of the successful factory, set up their own factories, too. Times were good.

Eventually, the factory owners' enthusiasm for production outpaced the stream of buyers' orders. Overproduction resulted in a glut of product. Factory owners reduced prices

Thomas High's Spinning Jenny circa 1764

to clear unsold inventories. They dismissed some Workers and reduced hours of operation. The money Workers got from wages fell even below the minimum subsistence, the cost of necessities. In some cases, the owners ceased operation and closed the factories.

The bad times returned. Discharged Workers joined the unemployed reserve. Having no wages, they had no means to pay for house rent and food. Landlords evicted many. Starvation and disease reduced the numbers of the unemployed reserve.

New orders for goods didn't cease but sank to low levels easily met by remaining inventories and the production from remaining factories.

A new machine would lower the cost of making product, often by more advanced automation requiring fewer Workers for operation. Initially, the owners had higher rates of profit with the new machines, even while the lower prices of product attracted more orders. A new period of good times began.

We aren't certain Engels knew the works of Sismondi who wrote an early description of episodic economic crises. Engels (1845) traced the repetition of boom and bust in the factories of England. He wrote

So it goes on perpetually – prosperity, crisis, prosperity, crisis, and this perennial round in which English industry moves is, as has been before observed, usually completed once in five or six years.

Later Economists also considered these fluctuations. Kindleberger (1978) asserts that any economic contraction of interest culminates in a financial crisis. He identified financial crises in England in 1772, 1793, 1797, 1810, 1815, 1819, 1825, 1836, 1847 and 1857, a list which overlaps Engels' career and tends to validate Engels' rough estimate. A widely shared consensus view developed during the time of the great wars, and the Professors began performing *The Business Cycle Goes Up and Down.*

The Professors, that is, the Business School Professors, studied the Tales of the Economists. The Professors interpreted the Tales and composed their understandings in the more marketable form of lectures, television interviews, books, panel discussions, scholarly journal articles, and other performances. Some of the Professors were themselves Economists, but that's another story.

The Professors performed in the business schools for the students who listened carefully so they could become Managers or Professors or Economists. Some of the students would become Supercompensated CEOs and would donate large amounts of money to their favorite business schools to employ Professors.

In the performances, the CEOs were Ingenious Innovative Job Creators, great leaders, and the vital sina qua non of the Society. The Professors published articles in the journals. Hoping for a kind of semi-impunity called tenure, many also composed long books, not uncommonly sold to students at high prices.

In our modern age, the Professors' collective repertoire ranges from the classic *Led by the Invisible Hand* to the recent hit *Quantitative Ease,* still popular at this writing.

As a historical note, while working on suborbital launches at Wallops Island, Virginia, circa 1968, I copied by hand from an original document, a scrap of paper believed to be an all-time greatest hits list, compiled, we think, by a Professor "Captain" Ed Murphy of Caltech in Pasadena, California, circa 1965. Per legend and rumor, at Edwards Air Force Base in California during the great wars, Murphy articulated the well-known natural law, "If anything can go wrong, it will." Further rumors assert that Murphy's Law was misattributed to Murphy (Joy, 2000). But I digress too far. All that is another story.

Here is the surviving part of Murphy's list:

...High Plateau [Topic unclear. Initial part of the paper had burned away.]

Growth of GDP

Corporations Serve the Interests of the Shareholders

Mark to Market

Led by the Invisible Hand

Inelastic Supply Blues

Total Quality Control

Looking for my Marginal Return

Debits on the Left

But we digress. People who wanted to be Managers learned many of the topics (at least long enough to take the exam). Managers oversee the planning and operation of Firms and the direction of Workers. The esteemed Professor Peter Drucker, writer of dozens of books, taught that the main job of a Manager was to choose, according to candidates' best capabilities, the subordinates who could best do the job.

The notion of Management originated early in the period of the great wars (Hill, 2013). Before then, there were masters, overseers and Workers. In our modern enlightened era, four kinds of Managers have evolved.

Supervisors: Managers who manage Workers directly.

Directors: Managers of Managers. Not to be confused with the members of the Board of Directors.

Executives: A small subset of Managers, typically no more than a half-dozen per Firm. The Executives have authority over all the other Managers of the Firm.

Chief Executive Officer or CEO: Equivalent to President. The most highly ranked Manager in the Firm. The CEO can tell any of the Workers or other Managers what to do.

In Engels' Manchester, each factory had a single manager, the master of the factory, usually the owner or a relative of the owner. The only other kind of manager in the factory was the overseer, something like our modern Supervisor.

Engels saw that, at the factories of Lancashire, in the course of a business cycle, to maintain or improve their profits, the bourgeoisie would seek to reduce wages or to get more Labor for a given wage.

In *Condition,* Engels wrote that the private ownership of property, lying at the core of the "factory system" or "capitalist system," caused the Workers' distress. Since higher wages reduced Capital's profit, Engels saw the interests of the Workers in direct opposition to the interests of the bourgeoisie. He saw that the state served the bourgeoisie who sustained and directed the state.

The Workers interacted with the state only when imprisoned or questioned by the police.

Engels predicted that the bourgeoisie would accord Workers no improvement of their condition, and that the Workers would, with certainty, wrest control from the bourgeoisie by violent revolt, for they had no other recourse.

Violent Workers' revolt to effect change in the treatment of Workers wasn't a new idea with Engels. Perhaps he had heard of the Merthyr Rising of 1831 or the Newport Rising of 1839. In any case, his writings usually mentioned violent revolt.

Engels' Berlin editor was the Old One Karl Marx. TOC (the Tale of Capitalism) casts these two as great villains threatening the Society. The two young fellows had hit it off from the start. *Condition* was first published by Marx in a series of articles. Four years later, they collaborated to produce the blockbuster *Manifesto of the Communist Party*.

"A spectre is haunting Europe," they wrote. *Manifesto* encouraged Workers worldwide to overthrow the bourgeoisie with violent revolution.

"In this sense the theory of the Communists may be summed up in the single sentence: Abolition of private property."

"The Communists disdain to conceal their views and aims. They openly declare that their ends can be attained only by the forcible overthrow of all existing social conditions. Let the ruling classes tremble at a Communistic

revolution. The proletarians have nothing to lose but their chains. They have a world to win. Workingmen of all countries unite!"

And capitalists worldwide did tremble and oppose the Communists. The *Manifesto* struck like a thunderbolt and opened a chasm in the social structure that persists even in our enlightened modern age. Engels, the scion of a bourgeois capitalist, had called out his foe. In the century that followed, capitalists, monarchies and empires fell to revolutionaries quoting Marx & Engels. In various regions of the world, some form of collective ownership of the means of production replaced the private property of the bourgeoisie.

In 1867, Engels and Marx published their collaboration, the immense book *Capital,* identifying "Capitalism," a term coined by Louis Blanc (Blanc, 1851; Schwartz, 2016), as the current phase of the evolution of civilization. The Old Ones Adam Smith and David Ricardo simply described the economic system of private property and free exchange by which they saw the world worked. Engels and Marx said there was an alternative. They called the existing system "Capitalism" or the "Capitalist system" and said "Communism" was an alternate and "inevitable" successor system.

Capitalists adopted the term "Capitalism" to describe themselves, their adherents, the Old Ones Adam Smith and David Ricardo (who had never heard of Capitalism), and the existing politico-economic social structure. Communists, said the alarmed Capitalists, were all those who challenged Capitalism. The Communists, said the Capitalists, threatened the civilization on which Society depended when they threatened Capitalism. Communism is the evil menace in TOC.

Marx & Engels predicted a violent proletarian revolution (though Engels wrote in his preface to the 1886 English edition of *Capital* that England might effect the revolution peacefully).

Notably, Marx & Engels articulated an idea that was then novel but seems quite natural in our modern enlightened era: that history has an economic basis. They said innovations in economic means of production shape social systems and the trajectory of history. But that's another story.

Our next chapter relaxes and refreshes the mind with the first part of a four-part intermezzo. We turn from the nineteenth-century Europe to the Tale of a grand Monop that emerged in fourteenth-century Europe.

9

The Eric Tetralogy:
1: Rents and Monops

A subsaga of the Tale of Capitalism

TOC provides a way to explain our circumstance.

Prologue

King Valdemar of Denmark and his wife Helvig of Schleswig had a brilliantly clever daughter, Margaret. After a 4-year engagement, at age 10, Margaret married King Haakon of Norway, himself 22. Margaret's brother and heir to the throne, Christopher, died young, leaving contentious the succession to the throne of Denmark.

On Haakon's death, Margaret outmaneuvered rival Albert of Mecklenberg (Margaret's nephew, son of Henry and Ingeborg, Margaret's older sister) and succeeded in installing Olaf, her 5-year-old son by Haakon, as King of Denmark and Norway.

Olaf died at age 17 of mysterious causes, whereupon Margaret became Regent of Denmark and Queen of Norway. She had a tentative claim on the throne of Sweden via Haakon, but the Aristocracy of Sweden had asked Albert to take the job.

After a few years, Albert attempted to increase taxes on the Swedish Aristocracy. The Aristocracy, disenchanted with Albert, offered Margaret a trade. Margaret sent soldiers from Norway who, with the Swedes, kicked Albert out. Margaret became Regent of Sweden and effectively the ruler of Sweden, Norway and Denmark.

Margaret adopted 8-year-old Eric of Pomerania (Margaret's great-nephew, son of Maria of Mecklenberg, daughter of Ingeborg, mother of Albert and sister of Margaret), brought him to Copenhagen and made him King of Denmark, Norway and Sweden.

Long before the Old Ones, Eric of Pomerania ascended to the Scandinavian thrones. His future held trials and adventures and triumphs, wars, the Monop shifting the benefits of trade to enhance the Firehose Up, the eventual grandeur of his kingdom, the woman he would marry, the woman he would love, his flight from the throne, and piracy.

Eric of Pomerania 1381-1459

In his Wikipedia portrait, he looks as though his lunch distressed his belly. He was known for his troublesome temper and marvelously good looks. He could be more charming than any Hollywood hero. Pope Pius II wrote "all women were drawn to him."

What is a Monop? What is the Firehose Up? Let's digress a bit, or perhaps a good long while, with what a Monop is, how it works, and where Monop Rents come from. But we will definitely resume with the great adventures of King Eric.

A Monop is a Monopoly or a Monopsony (depending on context) or a person who benefits from them. A marketplace having a single seller Monopoly has no competition among sellers. If a seller of a product is the only seller in the market, then that seller is (or has) a pure Monopoly because there's no competition among sellers. If there are about five or fewer other sellers of the same product, then each of the five sellers has a practical Monopoly.

In common use, very few pure Monopolies exist, but we can easily identify practical Monopolies in our modern enlightened age. When we speak of "Monopoly," without qualification, we usually refer to a practical Monopoly.

Within walking distance of my home, Home Depot has hundreds of different sizes and styles of screwdrivers. There are four other grocery and general merchandise stores where you might find one or two kinds of screwdrivers after hunting for a while. Within this little geography, Home Depot has a practical Monopoly on screwdrivers.

Similarly, a Monopsony has no competition among buyers. In my neighborhood, if I want high-speed internet service by wire to my house, I must choose between two companies. One seems continuously to offer a "promotional" price which changes to a higher "regular" price after six months or a year, and they will switch to the latest "promotional" price if asked. The other has a price that never changes and a somewhat higher speed. The price the buyer pays is about the same in the long run in either case, which of course seems high in the biased subjective view of the buyer. The service is about the same, though each has some minor pluses and minuses. The two compete, but not vigorously. These two companies are practical Monopolies for buyers of internet services. If you have technical experience in designing, constructing, and installing fiber-optic internet service, and if you want to find a job in this region, then you have a choice of these two buyers of Labor. For Workers, each of these is a practical Monopsony.

The manager of the only factory in a small town is the single buyer in a Monopsony. She gives up money in exchange for a Worker's Labor.

Generally, considering trades of all kinds, nothing distinguishes the buyer from the seller, except that the seller receives money. Monopoly (few sellers) and Monopsony (few buyers) have the same essential character. Monops have existed for a long time. King Eric established a long lasting Monop, of which we will soon learn the legend. Monops appear in the Tales of all the Old Ones.

We recall that in a trade, each of two parties gives up something they want less in exchange for something they want more. When a grocer gives up a tomato in exchange for money, the counterparty gives up money in exchange for a tomato. The buyer wants the tomato more than the money which he can't eat, while the grocer prefers money because she has more tomatoes than she can eat, and she has many uses for money. For each party, the benefit from the trade is the difference between the thing wanted more and the thing wanted less, a kind of profit for each party.

The Monop controls something scarce. The Monop can give up the scarce item in exchange. No one else can. Since the counterparty can't get the item from anyone else, the Monop dictates the price. A Monop grocer can price the tomatoes so high that many customers choose cheap beans instead. A Monop employer can pay the employees just enough to meet immediate necessities if they somehow get second jobs somewhere (Shin, 2013; Lubin, 2013; Nasdaq, Inc., 2013; Weissman, 2013).

In practice, some traders dominate their markets, participating in 60% or 80% of the transactions, with nearly the same influence they would have with 100% dominance. If the buyers in the market consist of five or fewer persons or firms, then they have much of the same market character as pure Monops, so we call them practical Monops.

Let us take a moment to consider Eric's and all other Monops. Ricardo's tale goes something like this …

The farmer's role is that of Ricardo's Capitalist who brings investment, her own or that of her investors, and the Capitalist's return is the profit. The farmer-Capitalist may hire Workers or perform some of the Labor role herself. For an insignificant ceremonial permit fee to the landlord, a shilling or so in Ricardo's time, the landlord can claim the land as property, and with the fee receipt the farmer can claim permission to use the land.

Good land becomes scarce if demand for product rises and the best land can't produce enough. Then farmers cultivate the second-best land. The second-best land produces less crop than the best land. Now the landlord of the best land can collect Rent, in addition to the ceremonial fee, from competing farmers, but the second-best land gets zero Rent, just the ceremonial fee. (The farmer and landlord don't know the future market price nor the quantity of harvest, so

Example Calculation of Landlord's Rent	Best Land	2nd-Best Land
Acres	1	1
Landlord's Rent Fraction of Crop	48%	Zero %
Harvested Bushels	40	20
Landlord's Bushels	19	0
Farmer's Bushels	21	20
Expenses of Cultivation	$30	$30
Expenses of Transport to Market	$4	$2
Expense of Ceremonial Land Permit	$1	$1
Price per Bushel at Market	$9	$9
Harvest Market Value	$360	$180
Rent Landlord's Market Value	$171	Zero
Farmer's Market Value	$189	$180
Farmer's Market Value Less Expenses	$154	$147
Farmer's Profit	$154	$147
Note: On the best land, if the landlord takes one more bushel for Rent, then the farmer would have more profit on the 2nd-best land.		

Chart: Daniel Brockman

they agree, when the plowing begins, to Rent as a fraction of the season's crop.)

Here, Ricardo spins the heads of his audience. If the landlord asks too much Rent, then the competing farmer tenant moves cultivation from the best land to second-best land. If the profit from the second-best land equals the profit from the best land, then there's no difference to the farmer between cultivating the best land and the second-best land. The landlord can collect Rent until the farmer comes to the point of no difference, but not more.

That is, the competing farmer will trade some portion of the crop as Rent to the landlord, until the Rent reduces the farmer's profit from farming a unit of the best land almost to the level of the profit of farming a unit of the second-best land. In this case, the scarcity of the best land (and property rights) gives one party (the landlord) the ability to transfer some benefits of the trade to herself from the counterparty (the farmer). The ability to shift the benefits of the trade is the key character of Rent.

The marketplace demand for product creates Rent. If demand for product grows to exceed the capacities of the best land and the second-best land, then the competing farmers will cultivate the third-best land. Only then can competing landlords demand Rent on the second-best land based on the market value of product from the third-best land. Landlords do nothing to produce Rent other than demand it.

Ricardo's parable of Rent ends here with competing landlords and farmers. Let's consider some implications for Monops.

The competing landlord can't get more Rent than the neighboring landlord for land of the same quality, for the competing farmer chooses the landlord with the lesser

Rent. But a farmer with a Monop landlord has no choice. No competition from other landlords constrains the Monop landlord. The Monop can enlarge her benefit from the trade by shifting to herself some of the farmer's benefit from the trade.

Despite paying high Rent to the Monop landlord, the farmer must maintain her level of profit, her benefit from the trade, to continue in business, lest her investors take their Capital to other ventures. The farmer may try raising the price she asks for product in the marketplace. If buyers of product will pay sufficiently more, the farmer restores her profit by getting some of the benefit of trade from the buyers of product.

The benefit of the marketplace trade shifts via the trades to the Monop landlord who collects the benefit as Rent. And if the buyers of product won't pay the higher price, then the Monop landlord can't get more Rent because the farmer can't pay more Rent.

Characteristic of Monop Rents, the maximum price the Monop can ask exceeds the maximum price in a marketplace of competing buyers and sellers. Another definition, succinct though pivoting on "dominance," is Paul Krugman's (2013) "monopoly rents: profits that don't represent returns on investment, but instead reflect the value of market dominance."

Workers taught their children that competing buyers and sellers bring happiness for everyone.

King Eric collected Monop Rents. Eric, with his shore batteries and armed ships, controlled passage of merchant vessels through the Oresund and the Denmark Straits. Eric increased the benefit of the trade to himself by reducing the benefit enjoyed by the masters of the vessels.

The next episode of TOC will continue the Tetralogy with the story of the Tea Party and the further adventures of King Eric. Oh yes, and the Firehose Up.

10

The Eric Tetralogy: 2: The Tea Party

A subsaga of the Tale of Capitalism

*A mythology, such as the Tale of Capitalism,
provides explanations and justifications
for the norms of society, inspiration and justification
for our actions, a narrative of transformation,
and perhaps a bit of entertainment.*

In our last episode, King Eric became King of Denmark, Norway and Sweden. With his ships and shore batteries, he would one day acquire and enforce a Monop (a Monop is a Monopoly or Monopsony) controlling passage through the Oresund and the Denmark Straits.

For large merchant ships, there was no feasible passage from the Baltic to the North Sea other than the Oresund. To obtain the safety and speed of passage that King Eric could make scarce, the master of a vessel had to pay Eric's toll, the Sound Dues. King Eric would collect Monop Rents, reducing the benefit of the trade for the master and increasing the benefit of the trade for himself. Eric's Sound Dues toll was intentionally small to avoid provoking serious opposition.

In many kinds of products, not merely marine shipping and the agricultural Land of Ricardo's Tales, a Monop escapes the constraints of competition and, within limits, controls the trade. To oversimplify slightly, the Monop names the price at the expense of the counterparty. The difference between the Monop's price and a hypothetical competitive market price is the Monop Rent, the benefit of the trade the Monop shifts from the counterparty, reducing the benefit to the counterparty and increasing the benefit to the Monop. Consider tea, for instance.

Most inhabitants of the Massachusetts Colony lived in Boston, the third largest city in British America. Massachusetts had no representative in the British Parliament, which recently had enacted the Tea Act of 1773.

THE TALE OF CAPITALISM | 77

British East India Company Flag

Until that time, the British East India Company delivered all its tea to London, where an import tax was imposed, and sold at auction to middlemen who sent the tea to North America, where an import tax was imposed.

The Tea Act licensed the company to deliver its tea directly to the North American colonies, where an import tax was imposed, but without taxation in London and without involvement of middlemen.

The Tea Act eliminated the tax in London, the expenses of delivering to London tea destined for the colonies, the middlemen's markups and transaction costs. Without these important expenses, the company could price its tea so low on the American docks that other sellers (principally Dutch and smugglers) offered little competition.

The East India Company had a practical Monopoly on importing tea to the colonies. Though the import tax was small, that and the Monopoly aroused much animosity among the colonists. "No taxation without representation!" became a slogan of the Sons of Liberty, a Boston political group.

One night, the Sons of Liberty masqueraded as American Indians and rowed into Boston Harbor. They

Cooper. Boston Tea Party. (1789)

climbed aboard ships of the British East India Company (chartered by Queen Elizabeth I as the first limited-liability corporation). They tossed the cargo of tea into the water, an event remembered as the Boston Tea Party, a foreshock of the American Revolution, but that's another story.

Long after the Boston Tea Party, a reincarnation appeared in Chicago. After the death of Reagan, clouds darkened the windows of banks throughout the world. In this time, the banks had lent money to many people who now lacked income because their employers, the Ingenious Innovative Job Creators, had dismissed them from their jobs. The dismissed employees stopped paying the banks.

For a long while, the bankers were certain all would be for the best. The bankers had bought puts. They had confidence, financial expertise, and many reasons why puts reliably rise when other investments fall. "The risk actually undertaken is very modest and remote," the bankers said (Lewis, 2007, p.29). Despite the confidence, sellers emerged.

In October, prices of shares on the Exchange hit a record peak, then meandered generally downward with fluctuations day after day for many months, a period remembered as the year of the confident bankers. In the year of the confident bankers, the bankers explained that the declines in prices reflected mere paper losses (Kiel, 2008). In the second winter after the October price peak, many mere paper losses became real money losses.

One Thursday that winter, television journalist Rick Santelli, reporting on current trading from the floor of the Chicago Mercantile Exchange, expressed exasperation that governments were giving money to people who seemed undeserving because they should have the wisdom and personal responsibility to provide for themselves. Mr. Santelli pronounced an unusually entertaining and memorable editorial, culminating with, "We're thinking of having a Chicago Tea Party in July" (Santelli, 2009). In these few words, Mr. Santelli breathed new life into the old political movement called the Tea Party.

In the Tale of Capitalism, we often find one term with two meanings. In this case, Santelli's Chicago Tea Party opposed taxes and the government giving money to people they thought didn't deserve it. The Boston Tea Party opposed taxes and the government giving a Monop to a Firm, which was different. (Incidentally, each week, King Eric's job included sending soldiers some place or other in his vast realm to suppress peasant uprisings and rebellious nobles. The chronicles are silent on rebel opposition to Eric's taxes.)

Some people, such as bankers and householders, urged government intervention to make good the debts the dismissed employees stopped paying, especially after some puts failed. Then, less than a month after Santelli's proclamation, prices' long meander downward became a financial cascade.

On March 9, 2009, prices on the New York Stock Exchange sank to their lowest level since the highest peak ever on October 9, 2007, having declined about 40%.

The Tea Party favored minimal taxation because, with less taxation, they would have more money to spend on cars

Nathaniel Currier (1846)

and houses in foreclosure, as Mr. Santelli had explained. They favored property rights, Capitalism, and minimal government.

The next episode describes the Staffs (yes, plural) more, but for now, know that each Aristocratic household had its own Staff of people to care for its Firehose Up, the household's income stream. The Staffs applauded the rise of the Tea Party. Property rights, Capitalism, minimal government and minimal taxation favored their work on the Firehose Up. If a Staffer did her job well, then she could describe increasing profits in her quarterly reports, which would please her Aristocrat employer, who would keep her on the payroll and increase the Staffer's pay. But a disappointed Aristocrat, much like an Ingenious Innovative Job Creator, could dismiss a Staffer from her job.

Property rights meant governments would protect the Aristocrats' Capital, so no one else could divert it by fraud or theft. Capitalism, of course, was the relatively new name for that confluence of marketplaces and private property that the Old Ones Smith and Ricardo had described, and the Old Ones Marx and Engels had named. The Firms owned by the Staffs' employers, the Aristocrats, were incarnate examples of the private property and marketplaces protected by the government.

The Staffs valued minimal government. Big government would impose laws regulating how the Managers treated the Workers. Big government forced them to do something with production waste other than release it in the convenient river adjacent to the factory or mine. Big government required they expose their accounts and explain their Firms in public disclosures. Government regulation required reports implying expenses of document preparation and handling. Regulation by big government helped sometimes, but mostly it caused significant expenses from unnecessary (because honorable Managers ran the Firms) work. We note that Smith (1776, Bk.V, pt.2) had written,

The acquisition of valuable and extensive property, therefore, necessarily requires the establishment of civil government. Where there is no property or at least none that exceeds the value of two or three days labour, civil government is not so necessary.

But that is another story.

Profits were the revenues, minus the expenses, and minus the taxes. (Technically, any payment by the Firm reducing the profit of the Capital is an expense, including Rents paid to landlords, wages paid to Workers, and taxes paid to government.) Not only did big government regulation burden the Firms with expenses, the Staffs explained, big government also required unnecessary government expenses, financed by taxes.

Without the "job-killing" regulation and taxes of big government, said the Staffs, the Managers might raise the wages of the Workers, and the Ingenious Innovative Job Creators might hire more Workers. The Staffs omitted to mention they might not. And, of course, expenses reduced the current quarter's profits the Staffs reported to their Aristocrats.

Per legend, the Staffs and the Tea Party fell in love from the start. The Staffs provided dazzling verbosity and graphs to the Tea Party. The Staffs urged Professors to perform *Growth of GDP* and other renderings about how lower tax rates increased government tax revenues and about how magnifying the flow of incomes through the Firehose Up, the Aristocracy's income stream, enabled the Ingenious Innovative Job Creators to hire more Workers. The Professors' innumerable performances taught that the Firehose Up conveyed GDP growth. Almost invariably, the audiences misunderstood by supposing the growth benefited mainly the Workers.

The Staffs arranged their client Aristocrats' political contributions so the Tea Party could get control of government. They arranged the charitable contributions to business schools to provide incomes for esteemed Professors. The Professors and the Staffs, having been educated by the Professors, provided intellectual allure to the non-intellectual Tea Party.

The Tea Party welcomed anyone who favored Capitalism, ideologists of the respectable William Buckley and Ayn Rand styles, Supercompensated CEOs, Aristocrats, the Staffs, and small-government Libertarians, because these people saw the unnecessary and undeserved expenses of big government.

They also welcomed survivalists, gun enthusiasts, religious zealots, nationalist zealots, advocates of unscientific points of view, anti-intellectuals, anti-communists, anti-immigrationists, anti-socialists, anti-abortionists, lonely people adopting friends' views, self-styled "conservatives," and other categories of voters who favored political ideas that wouldn't interfere with Aristocrats.

Together their large influential minority voting block had significant political power, with an intellectual sheen, and with the money the Staffs contributed. Tea Party members came mostly from the 90 Percent. In the Tea Party, the Workers aligned politically with the Aristocracy, the Staffs, and the Managers.

Every Staffer knew her future income could depend on the next quarterly report.

The chronicles tell us that on coming to the age of majority, the handsome, strong, daring, and impetuous King Eric of Denmark declared diplomacy had produced little, and something about "make Denmark great again." He made war for territory, draining the treasury, weakening the military, and ultimately losing a little land rather than gaining it. War for land would lead to his great Monop by sea, the principal component of his Firehose Up, about which we will learn more in the next episode.

11

The Eric Tetralogy: 3: The Firehose Up

A subsaga of the Tale of Capitalism

Our planet is much like the Tale of Capitalism, but not quite.

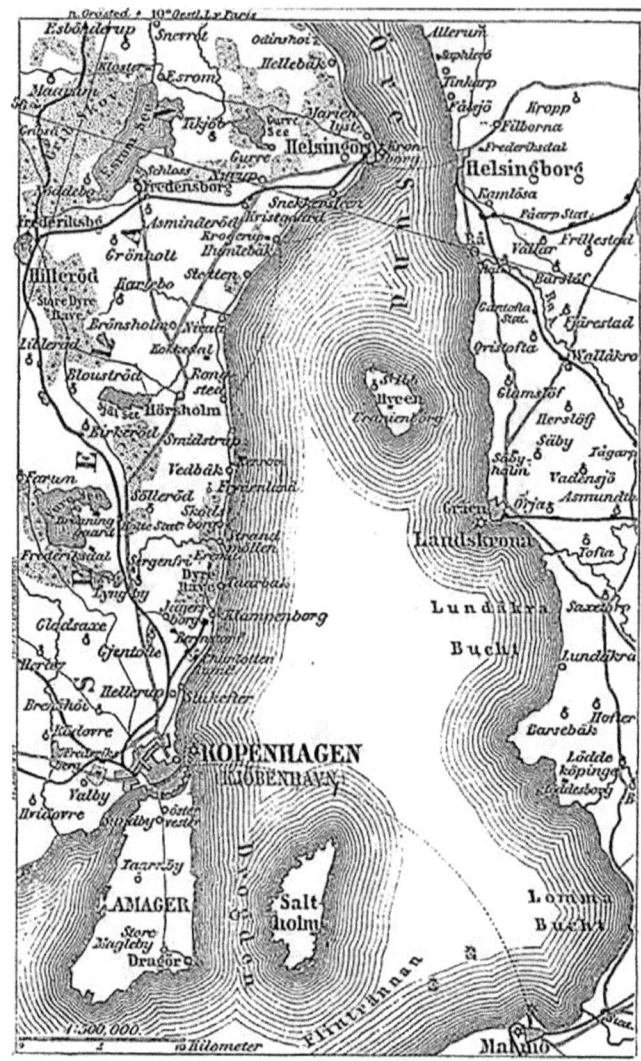

Oresund Map (1888)

In our last episode, we envisioned Eric's future Monop (a Monop is a Monopoly or Monopsony) emerging from a future war. We saw the Boston Tea Party disrupt the British East India Company tea Monop.

We also saw Rick Santelli's modern Tea Party align Workers with the Aristocrats and their Staffs to influence government. The Workers brought votes, the Staffs brought savoir faire, and the Aristocrats brought money. The Tea Party gained political power via seats in the legislature. The Staffs used that power to minimize government interference with the Firehose Up, the income source for the Aristocrats.

As you probably know, the Tale of Capitalism sometimes uses one term for multiple meanings. One meaning of "Firehose Up" refers to the intricate system of an Aristocratic household's incomes from Capital (owned properties and wealth), Supercompensation and all other income. The household employs a Staff, also known as the "family office," of accountants, investment advisors, business managers, lawyers, portfolio managers, and lobbyists (or contracts with providers of some of these services) to assure the astute management of assets, with optimal accounting and legal practices applied to the Capital and Labor income of the household. Thus, the Staff assures they can give quarterly reports showing increasing after-tax income from the household's well-maintained Firehose Up.

King Eric's Firehose Up evolved from ancient customs maintaining the King's property and incomes by the might of the King's ships, soldiers, and police. With centuries of improvements, the modern Firehose Up became a system of complex conveyances transporting portions of GDP and the greater part of GDP growth to the Aristocracy, with legal authority maintained by the might of the government's ships, soldiers, and police.

The other meaning of "Firehose Up" refers to all Aristocratic income sources as enabled and optimized by law, regulation, public policy, custom, convention, and tradition.

The story comes down to us that in generations preceding Margaret and Eric, after disappointing results from war, hard times befell the monarchy of Denmark. To make ends meet, the monarchy pawned southern counties. After a large part of these debts were paid, Margaret presented the pawn tickets. She wanted the lands back. Many kings and Aristocrats who loaned money to Denmark conveniently forgot the pawns and repayments. They said, "What collateral? Those weren't loans. Those were sales!" In numerous meetings, letters and conferences, she reacquired some lands, but negotiations continued tediously.

On coming to the age of majority, the handsome, strong, daring and impetuous Eric of Pomerania leapt to the saddle before touching the stirrups, like a western movie white-hat pursuing the bad guys. He declared diplomacy had produced little, and something about "make Denmark great again." Then he went to war to get the lands back. The wars drained the treasury, weakened the military, and reclaimed a little less land than they lost.

King Eric withdrew to long, sulking strolls on the cold, foggy beaches of northern Denmark. One annoyingly sunny day, he saw the bluffs of Sweden on the far side of the Oresund and a merchant ship moving through the strait. For a large commercial ship, the Oresund offered the most direct route from the Baltic to Holland and Britain. For centuries, pirates had waylaid vessels in this strait. In a flash of insight, King Eric realized, first, he could chase out the pirate riffraff and make the Oresund safe, and, second, he could make the Oresund a valuable thing that he and no one else had, and collect Monop Rent!

"Set up a toll booth!" Eric ordered an officer. He levied a clever toll. He required masters to stop their vessels at Helsingor and declare the value of the hull and cargo to the officer there. Eric's officer determined the Sound Dues rate depending on origin and destination of the voyage, the nature of the cargo, applicable treaties, bribes, and other considerations, but in any case, the toll took a small fraction, like 0.5% or 1%. Multiplying the rate by the master's declared value gave the amount of Sound Dues the master had to pay to transit the Oresund. But there was a catch. The officer could choose to buy, on behalf of the King, the hull and cargo at the declared value. If the master declared a low value or "forgot" to declare part of the cargo to minimize the Sound Dues, and if the officer chose to buy, and if the declared value was less than the master's costs, then the master couldn't repay his investors. If the master declared too high, then the amount of Sound Dues was high, then the officer took the toll, and the master kept the vessel, and the high toll reduced the profits of the voyage. These incentives kept the masters' declarations close to marketplace value. The masters grumbled and paid the annoying but tolerable toll.

The Sound Dues conveyed robust royal income from the merchants to King Eric's treasury. Eric used his possession of scarce feasible alternate trade routes to shift to himself part of what would otherwise be the merchants' profit from each voyage. Eric was a Monop. Eric was an Aristocrat. Eric had an excellent Firehose Up.

Monops dated from the most ancient times. A monarch (Eric, for example) or local gangster (also Eric, for example, as we will soon see) would protect an underling, making the underling the sole provider of some article of trade. The monarch would get a devoted ally and maybe an additional source of revenue. On the other side of this trade, the underling gets the services of some police or soldiers to suppress competition and the opportunity to maximize profits without limitation.

Elizabeth I of England

Monopolies emerged in grand style during the reign of Queen Elizabeth I of England, decades after Eric's Oresund Sound Dues got underway. The Queen granted a variety of monopolies. Interesting among others was what later people would call an IPR (Intellectual Property Right) granted to Tallis and Byrd to print and publish music (Chapel Royal, 2017). But that's another story.

Luridly and directly affecting matters of state, Elizabeth loved the 2nd Earl of Essex. No one could imagine why since his volatile personality made Essex the most ill-behaved courtier in her realm. Anyway, he needed an income, and she granted him the Monopoly on sweet wines, by which he received the taxes levied on the wine. When he rebelled and attempted to depose her, she came to her senses and chopped his head off.

Elizabeth ruled long before the Old Ones. You may remember, for the Old Ones Ricardo and Smith, competing buyers and sellers always existed, and so it is in TOC. However, some heretic Professors deviated from orthodox TOC with apocryphal explanations about Monopolies and Monopsonies. The more elaborate performances told how these existences were trivial or beneficial to the Society. These performances spun off a subgenre on "Natural Monopoly," referring to Monops for which the scarce good is a huge network, but that's another story.

Even in Elizabeth's time, complaints of abuses of Monopoly were heard in the House of Commons. During the decades before the great wars, legislatures began emitting general anti-Monopoly laws. Governments used these laws to constrain or take control of Firms acting as Monopolies.

Even so, Staffers would tell their children, "Wise children try to corner a market."

We come to the end of another episode. Will Eric find happiness in Cecilia's arms? What happens when ideas become Monops? Who is Cecilia anyway? All will be revealed in the next episode of TOC, the Tale of Capitalism.

12

The Eric Tetralogy:
4: Ideas as Monops

A subsaga of the Tale of Capitalism

*TOC provides a way
to explain our circumstance.*

Coronation of Eric of Pomerania

Who could object when governments, such as Elizabeth I of England and Eric of Pomerania, granted or allowed Monops (a Monop is a Monopoly or Monopsony) to their subjects, their citizens or themselves? Complaints did arise, as we saw a few episodes back.

The government receives the loyalty of the Monop, possibly taxes or part ownership, political campaign contributions, opportunity to trade on the Exchange in advance of news and perhaps some undisclosed deposits in foreign bank accounts.

The Monop receives suppression of competitors by the coercive powers of government. As with all fair trades, both parties gain benefits from the trade. Some governments, citing the peoples' right to pursuit of happiness, didn't generally require advance grant of permission to operate a Monop, so perhaps no visible advance negotiation of terms occurred, and benefits to the government weren't clear.

Each party gets something valuable in the trade by giving something less valuable. From where do complaints arise? While the counterparties to a trade do benefit, the trade may have pros and cons, called "externalities," for people who don't participate in the trade.

If your neighbor establishes a bakery on her premises, you may enjoy the "free ride" (positive externality) of delicious aromas when she removes bread from the oven each morning, though you may never buy anything. If your other neighbor establishes an unlicensed retail pharmacy, though you may never buy the wares, you may suffer the negative externality of strange people shooting each other in your neighborhood at all hours to resolve sales territories or customer service issues.

The Monop's customers and neighbors don't participate in the cozy trade between the Monop and the government. With each customer trade, the Monop gathers Rent, which diminishes the net benefit the customers receive. Their diminution of benefit, which Sam Adams called tantamount to tax, is a negative externality of the Monop's trade with the government.

With sufficient political opposition to negative externalities, governments acted against Monops. Sometimes, governments broke them up into multiple smaller firms, as with Standard Oil Company (Learning Network, 2012) and AT&T (Kearney, 1999, p.1396). Among other actions were monetary fines, regulation, mandated sharing of intellectual property or changes in operations, requiring compatibility with component parts from other companies, and disclosure of secret business information and software.

On the other hand, governments protected, even enabled, some Monops, like the IPRs we mentioned in the last episode. A government granted to an applicant an IPR on an idea. Of course, you know what an idea is. You probably had an idea recently, like today, and maybe it was "original," that is, no one ever thought of it before. You can't tell because you never thought of it before. For you it's just as fresh as if no one ever thought of it before. Even so, many of the ideas that any of us has were thought of previously by someone else. There was nothing wrong with using an idea thought of by someone else, and often much value in it. However, government could award an IPR Monopoly to someone else and make you pay the value of your benefit to the IPR Monopolist, or put you in prison, and thereby transfer from you the benefit of the idea to the Rents harvested by the IPR Monopolist. The government granted IPRs only for original ideas. If a person had an IPR, then government protected the idea like property, and no one could use the idea without permission from the holder of the IPR. Before governments began granting IPRs, anyone could use an idea, whether they thought of it themselves or knew of it from someone else.

With the IPR, the protected idea became artificially scarce, thus enabling a Monop. Before the great wars, the grand Monop J. P. Morgan said, "A man always has two reasons for what he does – a good one and the real one." (Wikiquote)

The "good" reason for IPRs was to reward persons with good ideas by giving them a potentially lucrative Monopoly, and the reward would enable people to think. Some people believed that humans had thought for thousands of years before IPRs were granted. The "real" reason, of course, was the IPR allowed unlimited income from Monopoly Rents.

J. P. Morgan

After the great wars, the most esteemed dean of the Staffs, himself an Economist, asserted (Greenspan, 2004) that "conceptual products" (IPRs) increasingly dominated "the economy" (GDP).

The Staffs acquired and tended and leased IPRs for their client Aristocrats, thereby increasing Firehose Up capacity, making more likely they could describe increasing after-tax income in their quarterly reports to their Aristocrats, and thus Staffers anticipated enhanced future personal income.

If 40% of the workers in a small town work for your company and can't easily get jobs elsewhere, or if you own nearly all the oil refineries in America, or if no one can buy tea unless they buy it from your company, or if 90% of all new computers won't work except with software sold by your company, or if every telephone call runs through your company's switching network, or if all the merchant vessels must pass through your strait and pay your toll, then you have a Monop, by which the Firehose Up delivers a stream of Rents to you.

As a professional courtesy, the other Great Powers didn't object to the negative externalities of King Eric's magnificent Monop, for they also had Monops to enrich their own treasuries and keep their wealthier nobles compliant.

Further, the monarchs tempered professional rivalries with nepotism. When Eric was in his twenties, his aunt Margaret arranged Eric's marriage to the twelve-year-old Princess Philippa of England. Their marriage continued 24 years. Then Philippa died.

According to one legend that comes down to us, love blossomed publicly between the recently widowed Eric and Philippa's lady-in-waiting, the beautiful Cecilia, scandalizing the kingdom. Seeking relief from the critics, Cecilia wed Eric with a brief pre-nuptial agreement by which she got nothing but Eric, which was all she wanted. But the scandalmongers persisted.

Ten years after Philippa's death, exasperated, Eric said, "Cecilia, the scene drags. Let's split." Cecilia said, "We can't. You'd lose the Sound Dues Monop and the throne."

Eric said, "But I'll have you." Cecilia gasped and threw herself into his arms.

He was heard to mutter something like "fake news," and off they went to Visby on the island of Gotland in the Baltic Sea, a centuries-old pirates' and smugglers' hideout. Supposing the ever-intemperate Eric had yet another tantrum, the nobility waited for him to return to Copenhagen. But he didn't. Eric took up piracy. The nobility elected Christopher of Bavaria to the throne.

Epilogue

Monops are components of the Firehose Up, conveying streams of Rents extracted from trade counterparties. The Monop gets a better price than would prevail in competitive markets.

Politically, Tea Party votes supported Staff efforts to enhance the Firehose Up, the Aristocracy's stream of income.

Royal officers collected the Oresund Sound Dues until, four centuries later, Denmark limped, diminished by wars. The Great Powers demanded and got zero toll for their vessels in exchange for a one-time payment. Likewise, the young government of the United States paid $400,000, which was less costly than sending a warship to Denmark (Hessenland, 1855). Made ineffective, the Sound Dues Monop ended in 1857 (Wikipedia, *Sound Dues*).

In Eric's time, a contemporaneous Silk Road bandit might have started with ambushing travelers in a defile, then building a fortress on a high hill to secure the takings, then driving competitors from the lands visible from the fortress, then establishing orderly customs houses for bloodless, predictable loot collection from travelers breaching the periphery of lands he claimed. He would end his life the greatest and most serene of kings.

But Eric lived his kaleidoscopic adventures in reverse. He ended his life a pirate commandeering merchant vessels in the straits and preceded that with a levy on travelers passing his tax collector in the fortress at Helsingor. Before that were wars with contentious foes, and he began his life as the splendid dashing Prince and King of the unsurpassed Kingdom of Denmark, Norway and Sweden.

In our future episodes of TOC, the Tale of Capitalism, we'll meet Ayn Rand and Karl Marx and tell the story of the Downward Trickle, the Aristocracy's waste stream.

The Workers told their children that money can't buy love.

Thus ends the Eric Tetralogy. Cecilia and Eric lived happily ever after.

13

Rand, Marx, and the Downward Trickle

The Tale of Capitalism is deeply, but inconsistently, sarcastic.

Once upon a time ...

Ayn Rand (1925)

...economics described the behavior of people as observed by the Economists. The Economists included Old Ones David Ricardo and Adam Smith. They set their tales in scenes of the emergent industrial age and described human behavior that they believed universal. Ricardo and Smith both recommended some changes of law involving trade and taxes, but mainly their messages described how the world works. Both were aware of the Downward Trickle, the waste stream of the Aristocracy, though neither of them called it that. The name arose many decades later in the time of Reagan near the end of the great wars, but that's another story.

Smith (1759, pt.IV, ch.I, p.127) wrote that the Invisible Hand guides the rich to divide necessities into approximately equal parts for all. Ricardo (1821, ch.31) wrote that the capitalist employs fewer Workers to operate the highly productive machines of the new technologies. "There will necessarily be a diminution in the demand for labour, ... and the situation of the labouring classes will be that of distress and poverty."

The capitalist pays wages to a Worker, seldom less than just enough to keep the Worker working for another week (Smith, 1776, ch.VIII). If the capitalist foresees an increasing level of transactions producing a higher level of profits, then she will expend more capital on materials, tools, and equipment, and Labor to transform these into product. The capitalists bid against one another for Labor, which raises the wages of Labor and lowers the profits of the capitalists (Smith, 1776, bk.I, ch.XI).

With greater competition for foreseen profits, capitalists produce more product into the marketplace. With more product available to buyers, the producing capitalist's profits decline, perhaps to the point of the capitalist's loss.

This greater competition, or war, or peace (paradoxically), or disaster, or introduction of machinery, or other cause may reduce the capitalist's expectation of future profits unless he reduces the cost of employing Labor. The capitalist then reduces wages or dismisses some Workers, eliminating their wages.

The unemployed Worker bids for employment against other unemployed Workers, reducing the general wage level (Smith, 1776, bk.I, ch.VIII, p.48), even below the subsistence minimum. Ricardo (1821) writes, "When the market price of labour is below its natural price, the condition of the labourers is most wretched: then poverty deprives them of those comforts which custom renders absolute necessaries." From this economic background emerged Karl Marx.

Karl Marx (circa 1870)

The Old One Karl Marx was a newspaper editor, educated, articulate, and active in the hodgepodge of socialist political movements of post-Napoleonic Europe. He read Ricardo and Smith, understood them well, and didn't dispute the main character of their descriptions.

Marx and the Old OneEngels met as young men and began a lifelong collaboration.

Marx & Engels compiled factual detail of the Downward Trickle of wealth and income from the Ten Percent (which they called the "bourgeoisie") to the Workers. They saw chronic hunger among the Workers and their families, with some starving to death during business downturns. They said these deaths were the unavoidable consequence of private property. Their analyses described how the world works, although our modern enlightened age remembers them mainly for their prescriptions for how the world should work.

A minor political party commissioned them to write a mission statement, the *Manifesto of the Communist Party* (1848). In the *Manifesto,* they summarized Communism as the abolition of private property, the phrase struck with the tranquility of a thunderbolt and caused modern governments to divide between parties favoring Workers and parties favoring Capitalists.

Marx & Engels wrote that the "capitalist system" (their preferred term with "capitalism" yet unused in print) was the unavoidable result of private property. Communists opposed the capitalist system. Communists called for the abolition of private property beyond a modest house, garden, storefront, and workshop.

The coercive powers of government defended the capitalist system, so that peaceful reform would never overcome it. For Marx & Engels, Workers had no choice. Workers would rise imminently, unavoidably, inevitably in violent revolution to replace the capitalist system with a new social structure featuring the control by the Workers over the means of production.

Legend informs us they were dividing the bar bill with some anarchist friends in a Parisian bistro just after Christmas 1857, when Engels overheard one particular word, which was the punchline of a wisecrack, the word "capitalism." The word capitalism first occurs in print on p.307 (ch.XXIV) of *Capital* (1867): "… under capitalism, where the social wealth [that is, the aggregate wealth of the Society] becomes in an ever increasing degree the property of those who are in a position to appropriate to themselves again and again the unpaid labour of others."

As you know, not uncommonly TOC uses a word with two different meanings. Capitalism, synonymous in

Marx's & Engels' work with "capitalist production" and "capitalist system," means the repetitive way a capitalist (person wealthy in private property) uses or invests her capital (which Adam Smith usually called "stock") and magnifies it.

The capitalist invests to buy MTE (materials, tools, equipment), and Workers' Labor. Labor transforms the MTE into product. By custom and law, the capitalist owns the product. The capitalist sells the product, possibly by employing Workers specialized in sales, in the marketplace for a price more than sufficient to replace the invested capital, and so leaving a residual profit (which Marx & Engels usually call "surplus value"), almost always money, and owned by the capitalist. The profit manifests a creation of additional capital. The sale of product replaces the cost of MTE and Labor.

In Marx's & Engels' view, the capitalist system doesn't merely replace the cost of Labor, it transforms a portion of the Labor, which the Worker gives up, into an addition to the capital, which the capitalist receives. Capitalism creates Capital from Labor. Clearly, Smith would have concurred, having written (1776, ch.VI)

"As soon as stock has accumulated in the hands of particular persons, some of them will naturally employ it in setting to work industrious people, whom they will supply with materials and subsistence, in order to make a profit by the sale of their work, or by what their labour adds to the value of the materials. In exchanging the

complete manufacture either for money, for labour, or for other goods, over and above what may be sufficient to pay the price of the materials, and the wages of the workmen, something must be given for the profits of the undertaker of the work, who hazards his stock in this adventure. The value which the workmen add to the materials, therefore, resolves itself in this case into two parts, of which the one pays their wages, the other the profits of their employer upon the whole stock of materials and wages which he advanced."

And succinctly,

"... the whole produce of labour does not always belong to the labourer. He must in most cases share it with the owner of the stock which employs him."

Capitalism also means a political view advocated by persons who favor the capitalist system, who may or may not have great wealth of their own. Political Capitalists emerged with the anti-communism that appeared in the wake of the *Manifesto*. Perhaps you can easily imagine a capitalist of great wealth might consider herself a Political Capitalist, advocating for private property and the capitalist system that makes her wealth greater. A poor person also can be a Political Capitalist, but can't be a capitalist of great wealth.

Skyline of New York City (circa 1950)

In the time of Marx & Engels, Capitalists and Political Capitalists influenced the governments. However, socialists and other acquaintances of communists successfully obtained laws over the next decades to abolish child labor, to limit the hours of the workweek, to legalize labor unions, to tax incomes progressively (higher incomes taxed at higher rates), etc. Many Capitalists of wealth and their allies identified themselves as Political Capitalists and organized to oppose the socialists, to preserve private property and to prevent impairment of profits.

A century after Marx's & Engels' midwifery of Capitalism, during the great wars, Ayn Rand wrote novels that remain popular in our modern enlightened age (her *Atlas Shrugged* (1957) ranks 66 on Amazon's list of Political Fiction at this writing) and hosted an intellectual salon of Political Capitalists in Manhattan.

Her nonfiction book *The Virtue of Selfishness* (1961) gives a lucid defense of capitalism. It may provide the most understandable articulation of Political Capitalism, including the anti-communist political movement. She performed like a Professor, but she was not one. She was not an Old One, nor an Economist. She evades classification.

Rand articulated what she called the philosophy of Objectivism, which has enjoyed wide acclaim. Objectivism described virtuous selfishness as the motive for private property and freedom.

Virtuous selfishness, Rand said (1961, p.11), was objective and rational much as Marx said communist revolution was scientific in basis (Marx & Engels, 1867) and inevitable (Marx & Engels, 1848). Rand conflated the tyrannies of Stalin, Castro, and Mao with communism and socialism. Stalin, Castro, and Mao were dictators. Stalin, Castro, and Mao were socialists and communists. Therefore, socialism and communism cause dictatorship, so the reasoning went.

Logicians among us might note that Stalin, Castro, and Mao also wore pants. Rand doesn't explain why the non-socialist and non-communist governments of Tsar Nicholas II of Russia, President Fulgencio Batista of Cuba, and President Stroessner of Paraguay were dictatorships.

Rand and other Political Capitalists asserted that Capitalism is or leads to personal freedom, despite the numerous counterexamples, including the previous three cases, Pinochet's Chile, Franco's Spain, the Atlantic slave trade, Ernesto Geisel's Brazil, Duvalier's Haiti, Videla's Argentina, and others.

Rand (1961, p.36) said private property was necessary for human rights. Marx & Engels (1848, pp.15,18,19) said the 90 Percent had no rights and no significant property, and that only the Ten Percent, the possessors of capital, enjoyed rights.

Marx & Engels (1867, p.177) said Capitalism, by bringing together large numbers of Workers who co-operated in the tasks of the enterprise, had produced wonders far surpassing the Egyptian pyramids. Rand (1961, p.105) said capitalism produced the grand skyline of New York.

Rand (1961, p.105) said Capitalism raises the standard of living of all people, and that inhabitants of the slums lead a life of luxury compared with an Egyptian slave in the time of the pharaohs. Marx & Engels (1867, pp.350-366) said the slums are where the Workers die under capitalism. Rand did not explain why slums exist.

The word "slum" was seldom used after the death of Reagan. Earlier, when the children of the Ten Percent asked "Daddy, what's a slum?", they were told, "That's where the poor people live."

In our modern enlightened era, the Staffs, promoting enhancements to the Firehose Up, describe how the Downward Trickle, the waste stream of the Aristocracy,

Pyramids of Egypt (circa 1900)

conveys a rising standard of living to all people. Parts of the usual rendering of *Growth of GDP* focus on per capita GDP, Adam Smith's promised equal parts for all by the Invisible Hand. As the 50 Percent pluck their standard of living from the Downward Trickle, children hunger (Coleman-Jensen et al, 2020, 2017).

In our next episode of the Tale of Capitalism, the amazing Invisible Hand will guide the Corporations as they frolic in the Free Market.

14

Corporations, The Free Market, and the Invisible Hand

*The first function of a mythology
is to waken and maintain in the individual
a sense of wonder and participation
in the mystery of this finally inscrutable universe.*

– Joseph Campbell

James Lancaster VI, commander of the first voyage of the East India Company (1596)

Long before the Old Ones, an ingenious new technology for organizing production appeared. In 1600,

Elizabeth I of England chartered the first limited liability Corporation, "The Governor and Company of Merchants of London, Trading into the East-Indies," universally known by the shorter "East India Company" (or British East India Company when avoiding confusion with the Dutch East India Company, founded in 1602). One hundred twenty-five shareholders contributed the initial 72,000 pounds of capital.

While some Corporations vary from the following description, and many differ in some respects, the significant characteristics generally follow a pattern.

The Corporation begins when the Corporation's CFO (Chief Financial Officer, a.k.a. Treasurer) receives something of value, usually cash or an existing business, from the initial investors. The CFO gives them ownership shares, each share having the same value. Each investor (now a shareholder, a.k.a. stockholder) owns part of the corporation in proportion to the number of shares she owns, and the shareholders control a limited liability Corporation. More or less simultaneously, the investors choose the CEO (Chief Executive Officer, a.k.a. President), who makes day-to-day decisions for the owners and manages employees, and a committee called the Board of Directors, which hires and fires the CxOs and decides questions on behalf of the owners.

Even before Elizabeth I, a Corporation was a more or less formal group of people, organized for some purpose and empowered by law to act as an entity or person. The Old

One Adam Smith (1776, p. 69) described the economic role of trade guild corporations.

Since the great wars, "Corporation" has referred usually to business Corporations, organized by investors, Staffs, managers, and entrepreneurs to raise a fund of capital, shift tax burdens, and increase their personal wealth by collecting surplus value or profit. In our modern Society, we use Corporations to supply many, perhaps most, of the goods we use.

Depending on current law, the Corporation resembles a person, because it can autonomously conclude contracts, trade, incur debt, declare bankruptcy, and contribute to political campaigns.

"Limited liability company" means if the Corporation gets in trouble, then it's the Corporation's fault, not the shareholders' fault. The shareholders bought their shares from the Corporation or on the Exchange. Their liability is limited to what they paid for their shares. Having already paid, they have no further liability.

If customers sue the Corporation for making a dangerous product, and the judge orders the Corporation to pay, then the shareholders pay nothing. If the Corporation borrows excessively and can't pay the debt, the Corporation pays what it can, and shareholders have no obligation.

East India Company Chop

That means shareholders aren't responsible for the Corporation they

Certificate for six shares of stock in a Corporation (1887)

own. That means the Corporation is a "moral hazard." That doesn't mean the Corporation is a bad thing. The big knives in your kitchen are physical hazards. They aren't bad things. We must be careful with hazards and knives and Corporations. But that's another story.

The Corporation's CEO, chosen by the Board, outranks other Managers. If the Corporation's surplus value or profit usually increases somewhat from year to year, then the Staffs advise their Aristocrats to allow the CEO a free hand. And if the Corporation's surplus value or profit declines too much or becomes negative, then the Staffs often sell their Aristocrats' shares to avoid the tedium of dismissing the CEO. Some of the Board may encourage the resignation of the CEO then give a newly hired CEO a free hand. The remaining apathetic and hopeful shareholders usually allow the CEO a free hand. Corporations owning Corporations and other ingenious legal elaborations of the art add further distance to the shareholders from the CEO. The authority of the CEO with a free hand may grow enough that she chooses members of the Board. But that's another story.

Generally, traders exchange the shares of a new or small Corporation in the Free Market, so that a shareholder can sell some of her shares or buy some more at any time a counterparty can be located. The shares of Corporations with many shareholders trade on the Exchange, a submarket within the Free Market.

"Whoever offers to another a bargain of any kind, proposes to do this. Give me that which I want, and you shall have this which you want, is the meaning of every such offer; and it is in this manner that we obtain from one another the far greater part of those good offices which we stand in need of."
— Adam Smith (1776)

In the Free Market, many buyers and many sellers compete. Any seller (or buyer), dissatisfied with a price (or product and price) offered by a buyer (or seller), can readily find another seller (or buyer) with whom to trade. When they trade, each person gets what she wants by giving up what she wants less.

Smith (1776, ch.II) observed that, when we as buyers approach a seller in the Free Market, "It is not from the

Market, Padua, Italy (1891)

benevolence of the butcher, the brewer, or the baker that we expect our dinner, but from their regard to their own interest. We address ourselves not to their humanity, but to their self-love ..." Trading is a public service distributing to all what they need. Each buyer and seller "... intends only his own gain; and he is in this, as in many other cases, led by an Invisible Hand to promote an end which was no part of his intention."

Smith (1759, pp.127,128) also wrote that the Invisible Hand guides an employer to distribute the necessaries of life in roughly equal quantities to the Workers, so each person gets an approximately even portion. But that is another story.

The Economists George Akerlof, Michael Spence, and Joseph Stiglitz wrote of information asymmetries – snakes in the garden of the Free Market. The holder of a product knows better than others the quality of the product. The seller of the used car knows if the car is a low-quality "lemon" or a high-quality "peach." The prospective buyer, knowing less, discounts her offered price to mitigate the inferior possibility of buying a "lemon." But if the seller knows the car is a "peach," then she hesitates to reduce her price. The seller's price exceeds the buyer's price, hence no trade occurs. Neither party benefits if no trade occurs. Each trader benefits in a fair trade.

When the CEO goes to the Free Market to hire Managers and Workers, information asymmetry accompanies each hire. The current employer knows the individual employee's ability well. The prospective employer discounts the wage offered the prospective employee, as Stiglitz (2001) says, "knowing that they will succeed in luring him away from his current employer only if they bid too much. If they bid less than his productivity, his current employer will match. Labor mobility is impeded."

And negative externalities inhabit the Free Market. When people of the same industry meet, even at parties and entertainments, wrote Adam Smith (1776, p.72), "the conversation ends in a conspiracy against the public, or in some contrivance to raise prices."

Alas, though in our enlightened modern era the Exchange and the shopping mall approximate the Free Market, we should keep in mind that the Free Market is a romantic notion, occurring in stories and performances as an ideal, but otherwise hardly ever.

Every serious student remembered when the Professor seized the podium with one hand, raised the other to the sky and thundered to the class: "The only purpose of a Corporation is the profits of the stockholders!" (*Dodge v. Ford,* 1919)

15

Capital and the Chairman

*TOC consists of anecdotes
confirming to some of us
that universal laws of human behavior
and circumstance imply our views.*

This story probably didn't happen, though it might have.

The Chairman – in our enlightened modern era, nearly all chairpersons are male – knew that, as representative of the shareholders, he set an example for others even here in the directors' private dining room.

Annually, the company paid him a modest few tens of thousands of dollars in director's fees for attending four meetings and signing a few reports. As one of the larger owners, he received several millions more in dividends, stock buybacks, and unrealized gains, of course. He put his napkin on the table, placed the napkin ring upon it, and stood up.

The Chairman's Staff had suggested hiring the man who was CEO, and the man had talent for his role. Despite the recession and declining revenues and dismissing 8,000 employees last quarter, the CEO preserved the company's rising trend of profit, the return on Capital. He whined unceasingly about the stress of his job. Still, this man's value to the firm far exceeded the couple of million dollars the directors voted to increase his Supercompensation, as they voted when the CEO whined every year.

The Chairman moved toward the door, with quick goodbyes to other directors. These were the faces of Capital. Some were wealthy individuals. Others represented investment funds, insurance companies, and non-profits. Several were chosen by the CEO, including CEOs of other companies. How predictable the directors! How predictable the meetings! How predictable the decisions, always consistent with the accumulation of Capital!

The Chairman was eager to get to Los Angeles for a swim before sundown and a good sleep before the predictable director's meeting of another Corporation the next day. The CEO approached him at the door.

"You visit Washington, tomorrow, right?" said the Chairman, hoping to minimize the conversation, it being perfunctory anyway.

"Yes, our industry is vital to the nation and creates so many good jobs for the middle class. I'm optimistic right-minded senators understand the stressful economic environment. I think they'll consider our indispensable service to the country and accommodate the unique characteristics of our industry by extending the research tax credit or otherwise easing our crushing tax burden. If they want more employment – and who doesn't? – then why tax the innovative job creators?"

"Good," said the Chairman, shook the CEO's hand, displayed a false smile, and strode quickly to the car.

Eight thousand employees dismissed last quarter, mused the Chairman. If sales increased, and the remaining workers couldn't produce enough product, the company would miss profit opportunities. If sales declined with further recession, then 8,000 dismissed might not have been enough. The CEO made the decision. Any of the faces of Capital would have decided similarly with the same information. The dismissed employees would grumble, but employees always grumble. They'll be all right. It was unavoidable. If Capital growth slows, then the capitalist must dismiss Labor to preserve the profit which is the growth. Growth is good. Growth means an ever more prosperous society. They'll soon have new jobs with new employers. Any competitive worker will get snapped up right away.

The Chairman's mind drifted to nostalgic memories of his time in Business School at the university. The capitalist buys Land, buildings and equipment. These were "fixed Capital" in the Business School Professors' renditions. The capitalist also acquires raw materials, parts, and small tools, stuff that gets used up within a few months' making the product. The Professors called this "working Capital."

The capitalist acquires Labor by hiring employees. If the capitalist can't easily find more workers to hire, then he can offer a higher wage or better working conditions than previously offered. Alternately, the capitalist can declare he suffers from a "labor shortage" and seek public assistance from the government. If the capitalist can find new employees easily, then he will reduce the wage offered new hires.

If a worker can gather the tools and materials at home to make, say, a table, then he can contribute his Labor to build a table for the use of himself and his family and get the full utility and value from his Labor. If, in the same way, he builds a second table and takes it to the market, then he can sell it in exchange for money, which will more or less suffice to replace the materials, compensate for the wear of the tools and compensate him for his Labor, and perhaps save a little money.

If the worker becomes the employee of the capitalist and makes a table, then the employer receives the money from the sale in the marketplace. From this money, the capitalist replaces fixed Capital and working Capital, and takes a portion for profit, which is his property, and pays the worker the smallest wage that will keep the worker alive and working through the next day. If the capitalist pays the worker more, then he must raise the price of the table or reduce his own profit. If he raises the price of the table, then he will sell fewer tables than his competitors, who will sell similar tables for less by paying their workers less. If he reduces his own profit below normal levels, then he will close the table factory and seek normal rates of profit in other businesses.

Every five or 10 years, manufacturers of tables and other manufacturers will come on hard times. It becomes hard to sell a table. The capitalist can't readily sell the full production of the factory, so he reduces the level of production, say by half. Reducing the working hours of each employee by half won't reduce Labor costs by half, since he must still pay some costs per employee. So he discharges half the employees. Our society confers authority, derived from government protecting Capital as private property, on the capitalist. He may seek counsel from colleagues and workers, or he can decide on their future income without them. So, half the employees join what the Old One Engels (1845) called the unemployed reserve, and what Veblen (1899) called the underfed class, or as we know it in our modern enlightened era, the natural level of unemployment.

The Old Ones (Ricardo, 1821, ch.5; Marx & Engels, 1848, p.7; Smith, p.46) described how wages may rise somewhat during periods of high production or for a few years for a few employees with special skills. The unemployed reserve tempers the rise in wages by assuring some unemployed worker will gladly take the job at a lower wage. In the long run, a worker's wage barely suffices to keep his family alive. If the worker is discharged, his income stops. How will he and his family eat? Circumstances favor families differently. Some go hungry.

[Note: About 11 percent of US households, or 1 in 9, didn't have enough food in 2019 (Coleman-Jensen et al, 2020), about the same as Europe (Smith and Meade, 2019).

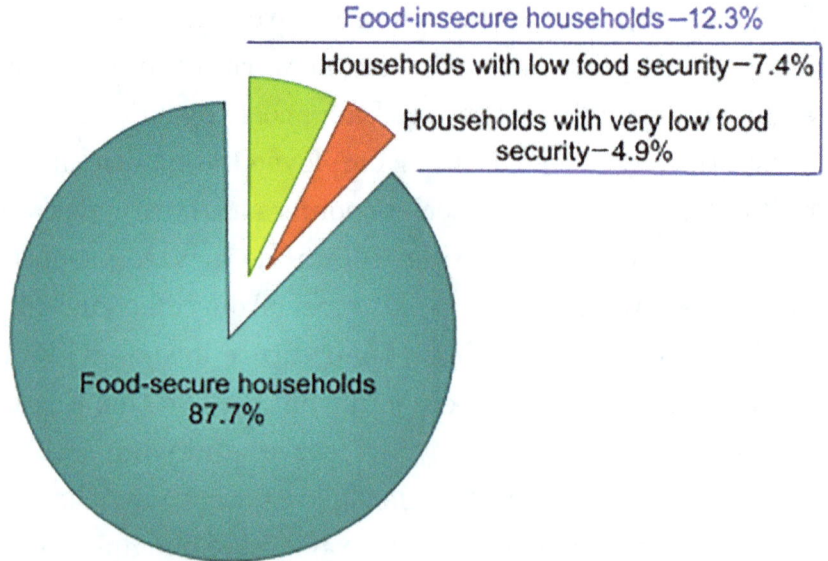

Source: USDA, Economic Research Service, using data from the December 2016 Current Population Survey Food Security Supplement.

Outside Europe and North America, about 916 million people hadn't sufficient food in 2020 (Baquedano et al, Jan 2021), and 1,200 million people in 2021 (Baquedano et al, Jul 2021). For reference, the population of the earth was about 7,800 million in August 2021 (census.gov/popclock).]

The worker knows when hungry people seek work at the factory door. As Engels describes in the "Competition" chapter of *Conditions* (1845), the worker knows it is better to eat today and take a chance on starving tomorrow, than to starve today. So, the worker agrees even to a wage that leaves him not entirely free of hunger rather than to no wage at all.

The materials, equipment and tools don't transform themselves into product. The worker's Labor combines with them to transform them into the product that has value in excess of costs, including Labor costs. The value in excess is the profit. In this sense, the profit is Labor transformed. The capitalist adds all the profit to his own store of Capital.

The Old Ones Marx & Engels told their Tale of the Ever-Repeated Transformative Cycle of Capital, the inexorable iron tendency of Capital to grow by transforming Labor into Capital. With each cycle, a portion of Labor transforms into additional Capital. The possessors of Capital always face a question the same way. They always make the same choice. Whoever they are, however bad or good they may be, they consistently choose to maintain or increase the portion of Labor transformed into Capital. Their faces are the face of Capital.

Arrived at his hotel suite, the Chairman changed clothes. Daydreaming, he made his way to the pool. One day, artificial intelligence machinery would substitute for employees, diminishing the wages paid to Labor and increasing profit (Ricardo, 1821). Capital would transform itself into more Capital. Robotic Capital would minimize the wage bargaining nuisance and bring spectacular economic growth.

The face of Capital glanced at the *L.A. Times* on the poolside table. "Thousands Laid Off," said the headline. He relaxed as he sank into the warm, oxygenated swimming pool.

It had been a long day.

16

The Old Ones and the 50 Percent

*Each person judges for themselves
the truth and meaning of TOC.*

The grandest characters of TOC (the Tale of Capitalism) are the four Old Ones — Adam Smith, David Ricardo, Karl Marx, and Friedrich Engels. The Old Ones wrote the most significant early Tales in immense volumes of prose.

You may hear Political Capitalists call Smith the originator of capitalism, as they often do, but they exaggerate. Smith sketched out economic components and profound economic dynamics that he observed in the state of the world around him, but he didn't originate that state.

Ricardo, Marx, and Engels cited Smith's works, disputed some relatively minor points, refined and elaborated others, and used Smith's terms. All four agreed in general on the nature of the economic system, which Marx & Engels named "capitalism" in their book *Capital* in 1867.

Marx & Engels articulated the political ideology of "Communism" in their book *Manifesto of the Communist Party* in 1858.

Smith (1776) describes how the wages of Labor merely suffice for the Worker to subsist. Under stable conditions, he writes, a man and his wife, both employed, have just enough income to maintain themselves and four children, two of whom die before adulthood. Employers choose among Workers bidding against one another for employment, and competition among Workers keeps their wages to a "scanty subsistence."

When employers expand production rapidly, their need for Workers increases, writes Smith. Wages may rise a little, a comfort encouraging some Workers to marry and

Adam Smith by John Kay (1790)

have children. If Labor becomes abundant due to expanded population, the introduction of improved machines or a decline in production, then employers dismiss Workers and wages decline. Smith describes prevalent beggary, crime, starvation, and death among the unemployed until the population declines sufficiently that revenue from production can maintain it.

Smith writes, "The liberal reward of labour, therefore, as it is the necessary effect, ... is the natural symptom of increasing national wealth. The scanty maintenance of the labouring poor, on the other hand, is the natural symptom that things are at a stand, and their starving condition, that they are going fast backwards."

Ricardo (1821) echoes Smith. "The natural price of labour is that price which is necessary to enable the labourers, one with another, to subsist and to perpetuate their race, without either increase or diminution."

The prices of food and necessities determine the natural wage level. And "when the market price of labour is below its natural price, the condition of the labourers is most wretched: then poverty deprives them of those comforts which custom renders absolute necessaries."

Marx & Engels (1867, p.271) echo Smith and Ricardo.

"The value of labour-power is determined by the value of the necessaries of life habitually required by the average labourer."

In the Tales of Marx & Engels, consistent with Smith and Ricardo, the capitalist advances Capital for equipment, for materials (Smith often makes little distinction between the money advanced and the equipment and materials, referring to them as "stock") and for employment of Labor. Labor transforms the equipment and materials into product sold in the market. The product fetches a price sufficient to reimburse expenditures on Labor and equipment and materials, plus a little more, because otherwise production stops. Since the price may vary with uncertainty, we may think of our "plus a little more" as the value of a Call on Profit because its value increases directly by the amount the price exceeds the costs of materials, tools, equipment and Labor.

For Marx & Engels (1867), our "Call on Profit" is "surplus value," the residuum after replacing production expenditures. The capitalist claims the surplus value (a.k.a. capitalist's profit) increases the Capital. Smith and Ricardo would have agreed fully. Smith wrote (1776, ch.VI), "The value which the workmen add to the materials, therefore, resolves itself in this case into two parts, of which the one pays their wages, the other the profits of their employer upon the whole stock of materials and wages which he advanced." And "... the whole produce of labour does not always belong to the labourer. He must in most cases share it with the owner of the stock which employs him."

Marx & Engels wrote (1848) the Society should abandon the system of surplus value, which is the transformation of Capital and Labor into Capital alone. Marx & Engels write that capitalism requires many Workers to live in conditions so desperate that some of them die, while the capitalist lives in comfort.

Marx & Engels fully agreed with Ricardo and Smith on the functioning of the existing general economic system, which they described in great detail in *Capital* (1867). In *Manifesto* (1848), they called for abolition of private property. A political movement opposing communism arose immediately that also opposed Engels, Marx, and everything associated with them, including, alas, people who wrote about them.

Engels and Marx became the high villains of TOC. By the time of the great wars, the political movement opposed to communism had adopted the name "capitalism," instantly conflating the movement with the economic system, and the members called themselves "capitalists," whether they personally owned significant capital or not.

In their *Tale of the Yeoman,* Marx & Engels write (1867, p.383-4) that the Crown granted nobles authority to clear their domains of families that had cultivated small inherited plots since antiquity. The Land clearing coincided with the invention of new machines, such as automated looms, centralized in urban factories where displaced country people sought employment.

Marx & Engels assert, with vehemence, that widespread poverty accompanied the emergence of employment in the factories of those made landless by the landlords who "stole" their farms by manipulating the laws. Of course, poverty long predated the capitalism of the 1600s. The Bible, Exodus chapter 23, commands proper treatment of the poor.

In Seville, at the time Christopher Columbus landed in America, the predawn of modern capitalism, about 50 Percent of the people weren't wealthy enough to tax (Fernandez-Armesto, 2007).

And poverty persists. In our enlightened era, the 50 Percent are the least wealthy half of Society. In 2012, Mitt Romney, the Republican candidate for US President, said 47 percent of the people don't pay income taxes (Farley, 2012; Moorhead, 2012). Most of the 50 Percent don't have

Income Distribution	
Shares of Aggregate Income	**2016 Money Income**
Lowest quintile	3%
Second quintile	8%
Third quintile	14%
Fourth quintile	23%
Highest quintile	51%
Highest 5 percent	23%

(definitions, etc.: www2.census.gov/programs-surveys/cps/techdocs/cpsmar17.pdf)
Source: US Census Bureau, Current Population Survey, 2016 and 2017 Annual Social and Economic Supplements.
https://www2.census.gov/programs-surveys/demo/tables/p60/259/table2.xls

enough income to tax, because (we may surmise) taxing the 50 Percent could raise political problems if taxes appear to deprive many constituents and their children of food. Indeed, some go hungry without taxation.

In the United States, 1/8th (12%) of households were food-insecure in 2016. 1/20th (5%) had "very low food security," meaning they didn't have enough food at times during the year for lack of money or other resources.

A fair trade, as between a buyer and a seller, produces benefits for both parties. Smith and Ricardo saw the deaths of some Workers as the natural, necessary, and useful result of a complex system of production and distribution that benefits the entire Society by increasing the wealth of the nation. Marx & Engels wrote, with outrage, that the customary trade of Labor for wages was unfair to the Worker; systemically unfair, partly because no trade could be fair when the death of one of the parties so frequently results.

Note: In 2016, the US Census Bureau poverty level for a household of 4 people was about $24k, which was, coincidentally, approximately the highest household income in the 20th percentile of incomes. Also, $24K is about the 2018 level of the US Department of Health & Human Services poverty guideline (determining eligibility for various government programs) for a 4-person household.

The US Department of Agriculture estimates, based on census data, state proportions of people in poverty, ranging from 8% in New Hampshire to 21% in Mississippi, and of children in poverty, from 9% in New Hampshire to 30% in Mississippi, as of 2016.

17

Growth and Income Disparity

*"The income disparity deal is real in our country,
and the question is,
'What are we going to do about it?'"*

– Bill Haslam, Governor of Tennessee

TOC is a dramatization and a comedy.

GDP approximates the total income of the Society. More accurately, we might say GDP resembles cash flow, that is, income plus depreciation. For most people, income and cash flow approximate each other. For the Aristocracy, they may differ somewhat because an Aristocrat, or the companies the Aristocrat owns, may own large amounts of depreciating equipment or property. The amount of GDP, average or per capita GDP, and rate of increase of GDP tell us nearly nothing about the disparity of income in the Society.

When we hear the news announcer say something like "GDP grew at an annual rate of 3.4% during the 3rd quarter of 2018," that's a big number for GDP growth, and it seems good news. The Professors discourse on *Growth of GDP,* a perennial hit. Politicians brag about it. GDP is "the economy." GDP growth is good.

GDP is Gross Domestic Product. People who measure GDP collaborated on the SNA (System of National Accounts;

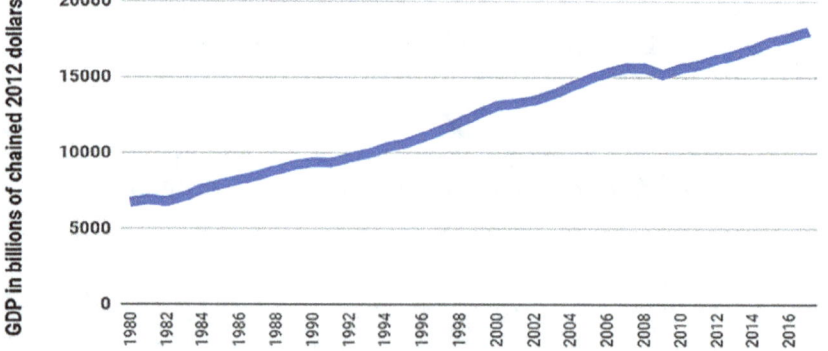

Source: US Department of Commerce, Bureau of Economic Analysis bea.gov

European Commission, 2009), 664 pages defining GDP and its components.

GDP equals GNI (Gross National Income), all the income of a national subset of the Society, plus the depreciation of capital equipment, usually about 16% of GDP in the US, plus all the stuff sold to foreigners, less all the stuff bought from foreigners (these foreign transactions adjustments net, plus or minus, 1% or 2% of GDP for the larger countries, though they may have more profound significance in smaller countries).When we consider the things that will make a big change in GDP or GNI, the main idea is

GDP = GNI + depreciation =
the value of all the stuff produced in a country

GNI = GDP − depreciation = about 5/6 (84%) of GDP

When thinking about the broad distribution of GDP and GNI in the Society, we want to keep in mind that, except for a few highly specialized circumstances, nearly all our decisions won't change if we use GNI instead of GDP, or vice versa.

For an accountant, counting up the assets, the remaining value of a large illiquid asset (like a barge or a semiconductor fabricator) is the purchase price less prior depreciation. Accountants deduct from income a fraction of the purchase price each year as depreciation. Accountants add appreciation to income when and if the owner sells the asset. But that's another story. So, depreciation changes little from year to year because it stretches over years. So, the more important changes in GDP from year to year result from changes in GNI — income, not depreciation.

GNP (Gross National Product) includes the worldwide income of citizens and excludes the local income of foreigners. GNP differs a little bit from GDP, but that's another story.

The news announcer seldom mentions how we distribute GDP unevenly. According to the World Inequality Lab, in the United States, the average real after-tax income of the 50 Percent grew 21% during the 35-year period from 1980 to 2014.

For the 40 Percent (the group wealthier than the 50 Percent and less wealthy than the Ten Percent) average real after-tax income grew 49%, for the Ten Percent it

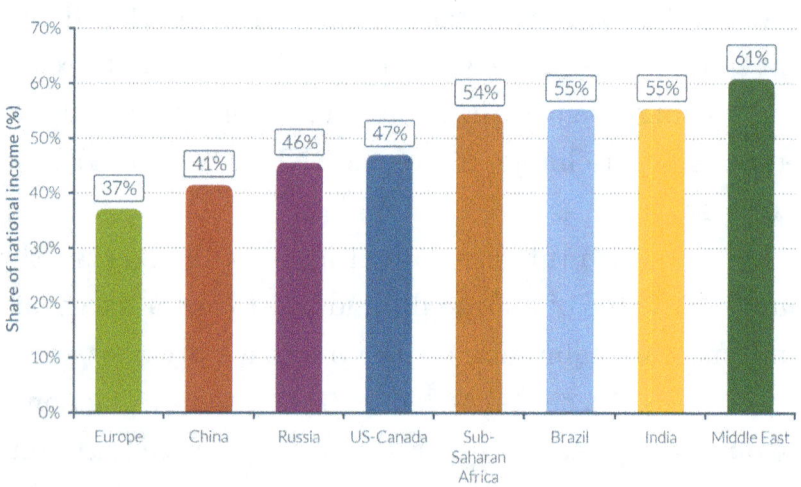

Top 10% National Income Share Across the World, 2016

Source: WID.world (2017). See wir2018.wid.world for data series and notes.
In 2016, 37% of national income was received by the Top 10% in Europe against 61% in the Middle East.

doubled, for the One Percent it tripled, and for the top 0.001 Percent, average real post-tax income increased 616% (six hundred sixteen percent).

Some people get much more income than others. We call this "income disparity." The OWS (Occupy Wall Street) movement circa 2011-2012 called it "income inequality," a phrase that caught on. The precise meanings of "inequality" and "disparity" seem in flux during this moment in our enlightened modern era.

Consulting the Cambridge, Collins, Merriam-Webster, and Oxford dictionaries, we find some definitions of "inequality" connote unfairness, conducive to conversational confusion over small, insignificant differences. Both "income inequality" and "income disparity" mean about the same thing, that is, a possibly unfair difference in incomes, with "disparity" disregarding insignificant differences.

From birth, individuals have differing talents, life experiences and desires, all of which shape their current and future incomes. As adult participants in the Society, their incomes aren't mathematically equal.

The differences among incomes are consistent, we may suppose, with the condition of our ancestors when they descended from the trees. If we can imagine ourselves there with them, one member of the tribe is good at hunting antelope, while another is good at sharpening arrows. Then the sharpener trades some arrows to the hunter for antelope meat. The sharpener gets food, and the hunter gets good arrows with which to kill more antelope. Together, they have more food to eat, and they are better equipped than before they traded, but they aren't equally endowed with meat and arrows.

A trade changes the distribution of goods in the Society, as it changed the distribution of arrows and meat for our ancestors. Because we struggle to imagine a Society in which the people don't trade, we can't plausibly suppose that the Society can maintain precise equality of incomes, if ever achieved. We haven't good reason to expect strict equality of incomes and wealth, ever.

Individuals find things to trade. For example, hypothetically, I could give you my seat by the window if you will give me half your sandwich. The possibility of a trade suggests a pre-trade inequality. Hypothetically, it is possible for a trade to eliminate an inequality, depending on specific circumstances. But, while maintaining strict private property, some conditions of inequality will evade practical resolution by trade. For example, if one trader has ten glass marbles and the other has one bulldozer, then they probably must resign themselves to some degree of inequality. The occurrence of a fair trade results in a benefit to each trader, but in practice, it probably won't result in equality. This diversion into discussion of fair trade again has led us off track. Let's get back to how we distribute incomes, GDP and GNI.

GDP and GNI in the United States being roughly the same thing, except for the Ten Percent who get the depreciation, we can map out fuzzily the distribution of GDP and GNI in the Society, plus or minus 5%, depending on the year observed. Thus, we see significant subdivisions of GDP by who receives it, and in TOC we call them GDP01, GDP10 (= GDP09 + GDP01) and GDP90 (= GDP40 + GDP50), the 2-digit number indicating the income stratum that gets the subdivision of GDP. See the chapter "Workers, GDP, and Economists" for details.

Income Stratum	Portion of GNI & GDP
Ninety Percent	50%
Nine Percent	30%
Aristocracy	20%

When GDP grows, who benefits from that growth? Recall the Ten Percent are the people with the larger incomes, the 50 Percent are the people with the smaller incomes, and the 40 Percent are the people in between.

During the 38 years from 1980 to 2018, in the United States, the Ten Percent captured about one-half of the growth, and the 40 Percent captured the other half, so the half of the people with the higher incomes got nearly all the growth. The 50 Percent got about zero, and some less than that.

In her book *The Divine Right of Capital,* journalist Ms. Marjorie Kelly calculated that some groups' slow-growing slices of the pie enabled the corporate profits slice, which

Share of Growth Captured by Income Groups, 1980 – 2016

Income group	China	Europe	India	Russia	US-Canada	World
Full Population	100%	100%	100%	100%	100%	100%
Bottom 50%	13%	14%	11%	-24%	2%	12%
Middle 40%	43%	38%	23%	7%	32%	31%
Top 10%	43%	48%	66%	117%	67%	57%
Top 1%	15%	18%	28%	69%	35%	27%
Top 0.1%	7%	7%	12%	41%	18%	13%
Top 0.01%	4%	3%	5%	20%	9%	7%
Top 0.001%	2%	1%	3%	10%	4%	4%

Source: WID.world (2017). See wir2018.wid.world for data series and notes.

From 1980 to 2016, the Middle 40% in Europe captured 38% of total income growth in the region. Income estimates are calculated usng 2016 Purchasing Power Parity (PPP) euros. PPP accounts for differences in the cost of living between countries. Value are net of inflation.

accrues to the Ten Percent, to grow three times as fast as GDP in the United States in the late 20th century.

The Staffs of the Ingenious Innovative Job Creators and the Aristocracy asserted that GDP growth brings a prosperous future. They urged lowering levels of taxes to cause growth of GDP, enabling the Downward Trickle (the waste stream of the Aristocracy) to distribute abundance to all.

In the early period of the great wars, in the time of Harding, the United States Congress lowered taxes markedly. A boom ensued, then the Crash of 1929 and then the Great Depression. There were significant income tax reductions in the time of Reagan and thereafter through 2017. Moderate GDP growth occurred, though at gradually lower rates than earlier when income tax rates were high in the period that followed the great wars. Ordinary fluctuations accompanied the moderate growth, then a big crash in 1987, and a recession followed.

In the 1990s, there were tax increases and an economic boom, followed by a big crash early in the 2000s, followed by tax reductions. In 2007, stock prices began a decline that became a crash in 2009, followed by what journalists called the Great Recession. After the crash of 2009, there were tax increases and a long period of economic growth. The US Congress reduced taxes markedly in 2017. Growth continued until the Christmas Eve crash of 2018 and the COVID-19 crash of March 2020, after which a period of economic stress ensued.

In our enlightened modern era, GDP growth enlarges the pie, but about a fifth of the people get less pie ultimately, only half the people get any additional pie at all, one tenth get nearly half the growth, and one percent get abundance.

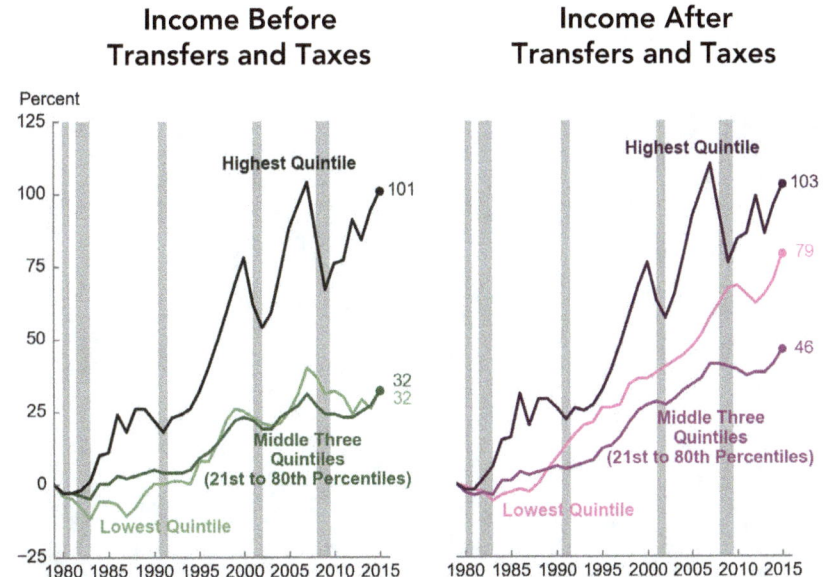

Cumulative Growth in Average Incomes. Source: Congressional Budget Office.

In summary, GDP growth mainly follows the paths of distribution of income prevailing in the half century up to our modern enlightened era and to all appearances continuing at this writing. The poorest half of the people get almost none of GDP growth. The 40 Percent get nearly half of GDP growth.; the Ten Percent get the other half.

Professor Younkins didn't mention Growth of GDP, nor its distribution, in his book *Commerce and Capitalism*, although his many contributions otherwise enrich TOC.

As evening turns to night, in our current Society, the Aristocracy lullabies their babies with "Competition among employers ensures that no one is underpaid" (Younkins, 2002, ch.9) and other lines from the performance *No One is Underpaid*.

Noah Webster, ca. 1825

18

Encyclopedic Glossary

The motifs of TOC, the Tale of Capitalism, give hope and validation to many people.

Aristocracy – a.k.a. the One Percent. As with many terms in the TOC *(The Tale of Capitalism)*, "Aristocracy" has more than one meaning. One meaning is the wealthiest 1% of the people. No one is wealthier than the Aristocracy. Some Aristocrats work and some don't. The other meaning is the 1% of the people with the highest incomes. On average, about half their income arises from their Capital, that is, the things they own and their investments in businesses, stocks, and loans, and their claims on the Labor of others. Their own Labor produces the other half of Aristocratic income.

Nearly all the income Aristocracy are also in the wealth Aristocracy, and 9 out of 10 of the wealth Aristocracy are in the income Ten Percent (Bricker, et al., 2020).

As a rough guide, in the US, we can estimate 2021 income levels. Based on figures from income tax returns (IRS, tax years 2001-2017 and 2018), the income Aristocracy includes persons with pre-tax income exceeding USD 600,000.

The wealth Aristocracy includes persons with net assets exceeding roughly USD 30 million, and their holdings roughly equal about 35% of all wealth in the Society. The Nine Percent have about the same aggregate portion. The wealthiest half of the Society has almost all the wealth. The 50 Percent have less than 3% of the wealth.

Board of Directors – *See* **Corporation**.

Business School Professors or Professors – The Professors study the work of Economists and of the Old Ones and of other Professors. They are experts of the principles of economics, finance, management, and related fields of study. Generally, they explain these topics well to others. They teach students, that is, aspiring Professors, Economists, Managers, and the Staffs in the character and dynamics of the Society's economic system and of the TOC (Tale of Capitalism). The Professors write research papers, books, and op-ed articles. Sometimes television news hosts invite Professors on their programs to offer explanations. Their explanations and teachings resemble performances. When teaching a class, they often perform a solo lecture from the front of a room of students. They perform a similar solo several times with different groups of students, as class membership changes with the seasons, each time polishing and selecting the arrangement of words best suiting instruction. Professors may emulate good performances by other professors. They repeat and modify the arrangement, like the troubadours we imagine toured from town to town in Europe's Late Middle Ages. We come to think of the topics of their lectures as performances, like the songs of troubadours. Sometimes Professors appear and perform as members of a panel of experts. The Professors perform renditions of the Tales and other stories. What most of us know of economics comes to us via the wisdom conveyed in the performances of the Professors.

Buyer – In our advanced era, a trade typically involves money offered in exchange for a good or a service. In these money trades, we call the two participants the Buyer and the Seller. The Buyer gives money to the Seller, and the Seller gives something to the Buyer.

Call – Traders at the Exchange devised calls as options to buy stocks at a stated price (the "strike price") before a stated future date (the "expiration date"). Let us suppose the following scenario. One day in May, you buy 100 shares of stock XYZ for $12/share. At the same time, you will be glad to sell your 100 XYZ shares for $15/share before October. So, in the jargon of options, you "write" a call, that is, at the Exchange, you sell the right to buy 100 XYZ shares from you any time before October. Today, the current price of XYZ is $12/share, so the opportunity to buy at $15/share has no value except for the possibility that the price will rise before October. That possibility has some value, perhaps $1.50/share. And that's what you get for the call. You get $1.50/share multiplied by 100 shares, or $150. The next day, the price of XYZ rises to $13/share. The person who bought your call sees an opportunity for a quick profit and sells the call for the value of the possibility that XYZ might rise to $15 or more by October, and let's suppose that person sells the call to another trader for $1.75/share, making a profit of $0.25/share multiplied by 100 shares, or $25. Since the current $13 price of XYZ is less than the strike price of $15, we say this call is "out of the money." In September, XYZ has risen to $16/share, and we say the call is "in the money." Several traders have bought and sold the call you wrote. The current holder of the call can "exercise" the option. The exerciser gives you $15 per share and the option, and you give them the 100 shares of XYZ. The exerciser could instead sell the option for $1 plus the possibility that XYZ will rise a bit from its current price of $16 before October. If the price of XYZ rises to $17, the value of the call will rise to $2 plus a little. But this is September, with little probability that the price will change much before October, so the option is worth maybe $1.01/share. Mainly, that is $1 for the right to buy XYZ at $15/share even though the current price is $16.

So, how did that work out for you? In May, you paid $1,200 for 100 XYZ shares. You sold a call option to buy XYZ for $15 and got $150. Now you have net investment of $1,050. In September, you sell your 100 XYZ shares to the exerciser for the option price, and you get $1,500. You have a net profit of $450.

That's the basic idea.

Warning: if you venture into buying and selling Puts or Calls for the first time, then keep your trades very small and few to avoid losing a lot of money.

See **Put.**

Call on Profit – An option, usually implicit, on the uncertain profit (revenue from sales less wages of Labor and other production costs) from the production and distribution of product. In our modern enlightened age, the Capitalist owns the Call on Profit.

See **Capital.**

Capital – Capital has multiple meanings. It starts as something of value, usually money in a bank account. The owner of the account exchanges some of the money for land, buildings and equipment (known as "fixed Capital" to the Old One Ricardo and the Professors) and exchanges some of the money for tools, materials, supplies and the wages of Workers (known as "circulating Capital" to Ricardo, and "working Capital" or "current assets," depending on context, to the Professors). The Workers combine the fixed and working Capital with their Labor, transforming the Labor and Capital into goods and services. The owner, the one who contributed the Capital, owns these goods and services by some combination of custom, tradition, law and contract. The Worker who contributed Labor to the transformation owns none of the goods and services produced. The owner sells the goods and services for money at a value higher than the combined costs of Labor and Capital from which the goods and services were produced. We call "surplus" or "profit" or "Call on Profit" the difference between the value at which the owner sells the goods and services and the costs of Labor and Capital. The owner owns the product, and the money for which the product is sold, which includes the surplus. From the proceeds of the sale (the money the owner got from the sale), the owner replaces the money used for fixed and working Capital, which brings the account to its starting level. Then the owner adds the surplus to the ending Capital in the account. In TOC, the provider of Labor, the Worker, has no claim on the surplus. The surplus increments Capital, the property of the owner of the account.

Capitalism – Capitalism is a word of multiple meanings. The process by which the owner of Capital (the Capitalist), dependent on the government's defense of private property, invests her or his Capital in expectation of replacing the invested Capital and receiving the surplus as an increment of her or his Capital. Until 1848, the process had been described by the Old Ones Smith and Ricardo, and it was widely regarded as the unremarkable, undifferentiated natural condition of humanity. A differentiation attended the publication of the *Communist Manifesto* (1848) by the Old Ones Engels and Marx, which called for the abolition of private property. The *Manifesto* struck like a thunderbolt splitting a great tree, the twin remnants surviving to this day. The *Manifesto* divided political and economic thought into both Communism, which was a splinter of Socialism, and what eventually became known as Capitalism, which described both (a) the Capital-Labor-Capital transformation process of incrementing Capital and (b) the political anti-Communism movement. Marx himself may have been the first writer to use "Capitalism," which he named in his widely sold, little-read book *Capital* (1867), in a chapter on the conversion of surplus value into Capital (chapter XXIV). He used it as a synonym of what he called the "capitalist system." However, the word "Capitalism" didn't enter common parlance until about 1900.

See **Socialism** and **Downward Trickle.**

Capitalist – *See* **Capitalism.**

Capitalist's Fallacy – *See* **Socialism**.

CEO – *See* **Chief Executive Officer**.

Chairman – We could refer to this person as the Chairwoman or Chairperson or Chair. In our enlightened modern age, however, the Chairperson is still, quaintly and almost always, a man. The Chairperson presides over the Board of Directors.
   See **Corporation**.

Chief Executive Officer or CEO – a.k.a. President, the CEO is the manager who outranks all other Managers and Workers in a Firm. The CEO works to improve the Shareholders' part of GDP10, and incidentally the CEO's part of GDP10.

Conflict of interest – *A preposterously unlikely scenario in which the employee of a financial firm who could earn ungodly amounts of money by acting against a client's best interest might proceed to do exactly that. Conflicts of interest are pervasive, if not universal, on Wall Street.*
– Jason Zweig, 2015

Corporation – In 1600, Elizabeth I of England chartered the first modern limited liability business Corporation, the East India Company. A Corporation is a collaboration among Shareholders, each Shareholder possessing one or more shares. The early Corporations varied markedly from one to another, having no well-exercised precedent. Smith (1776, Bk.5) describes a number of the Corporations that emerged in the 200 years after 1600. We present here a general description of the Corporation in the form to which it has evolved in our modern enlightened age. Specific Corporations may present exceptions in various respects. Each share is a receipt for money contributed to the Corporation, showing the holder is a fractional owner of the Corporation. Each Share has equal value and one vote in matters of concern to the owners. The Shareholders appoint the Board of Directors, a committee of their number, to oversee the activities of the Corporation. The Board of Directors choose the principal officers of the Corporation. The Corporation resembles a person. The Corporation, by acts of its officers, can autonomously conclude contracts, trade, incur debt, declare bankruptcy, and contribute to political campaigns. If the Corporation can't pay its debts or fulfill contracts, then by law the Shareholders aren't responsible.

Curve of Laffer – An ingenious explanation of the relationship between income tax rates, the growth of GDP, and the magnitude of government revenues. During the time of Reagan, the Economist Arthur Betz Laffer sketched the graphic Curve of Laffer on a paper napkin during a lunch with Dick Cheney and Donald Rumsfeld. Rumsfeld claimed to retain the original napkin in his private collection.

The Curve shows that if the rate of income taxation is zero, then government revenues are zero because there is no tax, and if the rate is 100%, then government revenues are zero or nearly zero because nobody wants to observably produce income because the government would take it all.

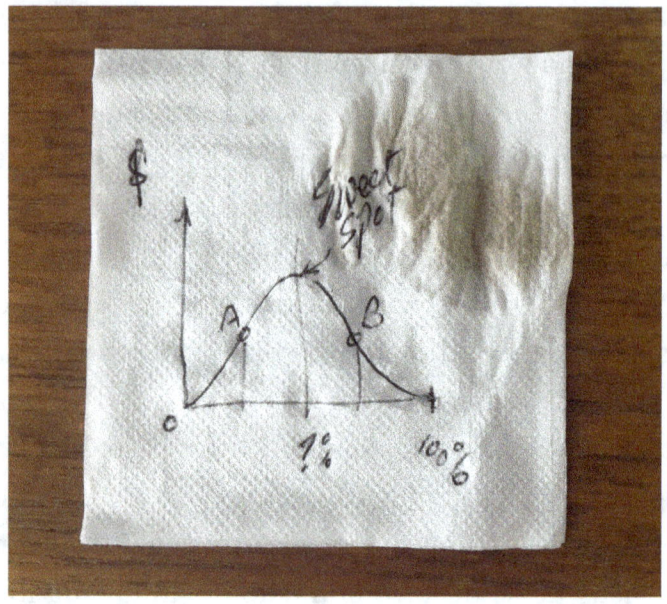

The Curve of Laffer (artist's reconstruction) 2020

But if the tax rate is somewhere in between, then people have incentive to make more money because a tax rate between zero and 100% doesn't completely disincentivize them. There is some tax rate, called the Sweet Spot, not too low (like point A on the graph) and not too high (like point B), which maximizes government revenues. So, from point B on the graph, government revenues would increase if the tax rate was decreased! The decrease in tax rate would incentivize businesses and stimulate the growth of GDP. That growth in GDP would imply more income to tax. That additional income and associated tax would more than make up for the decline in the tax rate. The increase in tax revenues would eliminate the fiscal deficit and reduce the national debt. Incentivized businesses would prosper, and the Downward Trickle would distribute the prosperity to everyone. Cheney, Rumsfeld, and Laffer went to Reagan, the leader of their political party, the Tea Party, then known as the GOP. They showed Reagan the graph and persuaded him the Sweet Spot was probably near 5%. In accordance with the Curve of Laffer, Reagan worked to reduce the top marginal income tax rate. The principal opposition party, the Dems, preferred an increased tax rate, but the legislature voted for a lower tax. Government revenues didn't increase, they fell. National debt and fiscal deficit increased. Businesses did undertake some marginal projects they wouldn't have ventured at a higher rate. GDP accelerated for about a year. On Black Monday, October 19, 1987, the prices of stocks on the Exchange crashed, and growth of GDP subsequently declined. After Reagan, the great wars ended. The fiscal deficit continued, aggravated by a new war in Iraq. With chagrin, the Tea Party, that is, the GOP, raised the tax rate. GDP remained sluggish. Unemployment was a problem. The Dems won elections and raised the tax rate. Resulting budget surpluses suggested the Sweet Spot was probably greater than 30%. GDP rose. Unemployment fell. The national fiscal deficit became a surplus. The Tea Party, still known widely as the GOP, regained power and reduced the tax rate, in accordance with the Curve of Laffer, to increase government revenues. The legislature voted to invade Afghanistan and Iraq (for the second time in a generation), and the fiscal surplus became deficit, and the prices on the Exchange crashed in the DotCom Crash of October 9, 2002, followed by higher unemployment and sluggish growth of GDP. The prices of shares on the Exchange peaked on October 9, 2007, and began a slow decline.

    A financial crisis ensued. Journalist Rick Santelli of CNBC revived the old name Tea Party on February 19, 2009, exciting spirits in the GOP. Exchange prices hit bottom on March 9, 2009, about 6 weeks after the Dems took power. The Great Recession emerged. Unemployment was extensive in 2009 but waned slowly thereafter. GDP grew throughout this time of the Dems. Dem political power didn't suffice to raise the top marginal tax rate until 2012 when the rate increased to 40%. With the continuing wars, deficits continued. GDP rose to record levels. Exchange prices rose to record levels. Unemployment declined steadily. The Tea Party regained power, declaring themselves alternately the GOP and the Trump Party. In accordance with the Curve of Laffer, in December 2017, they reduced the income tax rate sharply for businesses and Aristocrats. Unemployment continued to decline. GDP grew. Exchange prices rose to record highs, then tumbled in the Christmas Present MiniCrash of December 24, 2018. Exchange prices recovered over the next year to new highs, GDP grew and unemployment declined to levels not seen since the late 1990s. Exchange prices fell about one-third in the Great Trump Crash of March 23, 2020, losing all the value gained since the Tea Party assumed power in 2017. Even in our enlightened modern era, you may hear from time to time a Professor or Economist, sympathetic to the Tea Party, declare the Sweet Spot lies not at the current

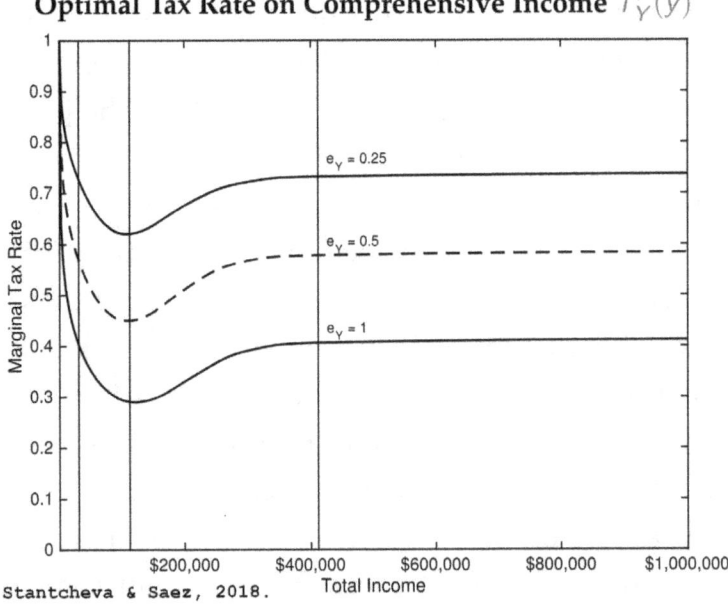

Dotted line estimates the Sweet Spot.

top marginal rate, nor at a higher top marginal rate, but at a lower top marginal tax rate, and that reducing the top marginal tax rate to around 5%, in accordance with the Curve of Laffer, will produce a fiscal surplus, businesses will prosper, and the Downward Trickle will distribute the prosperity to everyone. The Dems, however, seem willing to agree the Sweet Spot lies somewhere around 55 to 65%.

Depreciation – If you buy a big truck for use in your business, your accountant will want to depreciate the truck to properly recognize your income from the business. Generally, the accountant will recognize expenses during the year when a sale occurs to associate the related income (sale minus related expense) with the sale. Allocating the cost of a tool to a set of many sales of various products can defeat any effort to do so. Consider a big truck, for instance, used over several years to haul materials to the plant, to haul product to distributors, to haul office equipment from vendors, and to pick up pizza for a staff party. You and your accountant know you used the truck in the first year of its useful life to make products sold during that year and the subsequent year or two, and you used it during the second year of its life to make and sell products sold in the second year, etc. So, the accountant proposes to spread the purchase price of the truck over 5 years of assumed useful life by taking 1/5 of the purchase price as depreciation expense in each of those years. You paid out the money for the truck at the beginning of the first year, and you subtracted 1/5 of that money from total sales in each of the next five years. Suppose the price of the truck was $250k, paid at the beginning of year 1. Suppose your sales were

$850k in year 1, $800k in year 2, $900k in year 3, $850k in year 4 and $875k in year 5.

Your accountant subtracts $50k (1/5 of $250k) for depreciation of the truck in each year. Your income in the five years equals sales, minus truck depreciation, minus other expenses. Your sales minus truck depreciation (ignoring other costs) are

$800k ($850k less $50k depreciation) in year 1, $750k in year 2, $850k in year 3, $800k in year 4, and $825k in year 5.

That's the basic idea.

Directors – The Tale of Capitalism includes two meanings of "Director." The first meaning is a level of Management. A Director is a Manager of Managers, though the Director usually isn't an Executive. In the second meaning, a Director is a member of the Board of Directors that oversees the activities of a Corporation. Often, the Directors are nominated by the nominating committee of the Board of Directors. The shareholders elect the nominees because shareholders vote against the Board of Directors only in rare circumstances. The nominating committee, and the entire Board for that matter, are usually chosen from among the friends of the CEO, the Supercompensated CEOs of other Corporations and from the spouses, children, nieces and nephews, siblings, paramours, and significant others of the Directors.

See **Corporation**.

Downward Trickle – The waste stream of the Aristocracy, from which the 50 Percent may pluck a subsistence and an occasional boon. The Downward Trickle results from natural inefficiencies in the Firehose Up. The Staffs work to improve the Firehose Up, which includes mitigating the Downward Trickle. The Old Ones knew of the Downward Trickle, though they didn't call it by that name. Political Capitalists and Staffs often laud the Downward Trickle when seeking reduced taxes for the Aristocracy or less stringent regulation of their businesses. They say, as did Ayn Rand, that the Downward Trickle of Capitalism raises the standard of living of all people.

See **Firehose Up**.

Economists – Composers of Tales. Professors sometimes created tales, and sometimes other members of Society created tales, but Economists originated most of the Tales. The Old Ones wrote a few early Tales that became enduring classics.

Engels, Friedrich – Sometimes called the "forgotten" Old One, Engels was Karl Marx's lifelong collaborator and principal financial supporter. His book, *The Condition of the Working Class in England* (1845), describes the English industrial revolution in detail. It also advocates for better treatment of Workers by their employers, the Ingenious Innovative Job Creators. Engels collaborated with Marx on the *Manifesto* (1848) and edited Marx's grand work *Capital* (1867) to which he likely contributed some sections. After Marx's death, Engels completed the last volume of *Capital* from Marx's notes. Engels remained an active Socialist until his death in 1895.

Exchange – A big building housing a club of members who, acting on behalf of other persons for a fee, buy, and sell shares of Firms "listed" on the Exchange. In our enlightened modern age, some members' fees charged to the general public have diminished to zero, a nice round figure popular with the public, and a "Free Lunch" in the argot of the Exchange, but that's another story. The Exchange is a Monop, de jure or de facto. If the Executives of a Firm wish to "go public," that is, to sell shares of the Firm to the public, they deliver the shares to several of the members of the Exchange, and the members, for a fee, "list" the Firm and sell the shares to other members who, for a fee, buy the shares on behalf of persons in the general public. Sometimes Firm A acquires Firm B, in which case, Firm A buys all or most of the shares of Firm B, and the Exchange "delists" shares of Firm B, and the members of the Exchange no longer buy and sell the shares of Firm B.

Executives – A small subset of Managers, typically no more than a half-dozen per Firm. The Executives are the most highly ranked employees. They include persons with titles such as Chief Executive Officer (CEO), President, Chief Operating Officer (COO), Vice President (VP), Chief Administrative Officer (CAO), Controller, Chief Technology Officer (CTO), Chief Financial Officer (CFO), Treasurer, and generally any Manager who reports directly to the President or CEO. The Executives have authority over all the other Managers of the Firm.

50 Percent – The least wealthy half of the Society.

Firehose Up – One meaning of Firehose Up refers to the Aristocratic household's flow of overall income from Capital (owned properties and wealth), Supercompensation, and all other income.

A second meaning of Firehose Up is the modern system of complex conveyances transporting portions of GDP and the greater part of GDP growth to the Aristocracy, with legal authority maintained by the might of the government's ships, soldiers and police.

A third meaning of Firehose Up refers to all Aristocrats' sources of overall income as enabled and optimized by law, regulation, public policy, custom, convention, and tradition.

See **Downward Trickle.**

Firm – The Society organized itself into groups called Firms to find, gather, produce, and distribute stuff. Circa 1600, a social structure, the limited liability Corporation, emerged that eventually established a pattern of organization and behavior for Firms generally. In our modern enlightened era, nearly all Firms, enterprises large and small, even partnerships, sole proprietorships, private clubs, and non-profit organizations organize themselves much like Corporations.

Free Market – In the Free Market, many buyers and many sellers compete. Any seller (or buyer), dissatisfied with a price (or product and price) offered by a buyer (or seller), can readily find another seller (or buyer) with whom to fairly trade. The "Unfettered Free Market" has no regulation except by voluntary cooperation of the participants. Black markets in contraband have no regulation under the laws of a nation state and so resemble the UFM. However, some participants in black markets may exercise coercive regulation of other participants. The Unfettered Free Market sometimes suffers from bandits, frauds, and Monops who diminish competition or defeat the buyers' and sellers' possession of the goods and services they trade, or defeat fair trades. Hence the Unfettered Free Market (when approximated, as sometimes occurs) soon ceases to be a Free Market. Regulators and inspectors, usually provided by Governments, monitor Free Markets to assure safety, to prevent abuses, to assure legitimate pricing, and to enforce rules to prevent harmful asymmetries of information.

GDP – *See* **Gross Domestic Product.**

Government – The dominant coercive power in any region or other situation of potential contention. Because the dominant coercive power can argue with force, government decides the prevailing law and influences economic organization, taxes, and regulation. The extent of dominance of a government is its jurisdiction. The jurisdiction may be indistinctly defined in multiple dimensions, one of which usually is geographic. Government is inevitable because

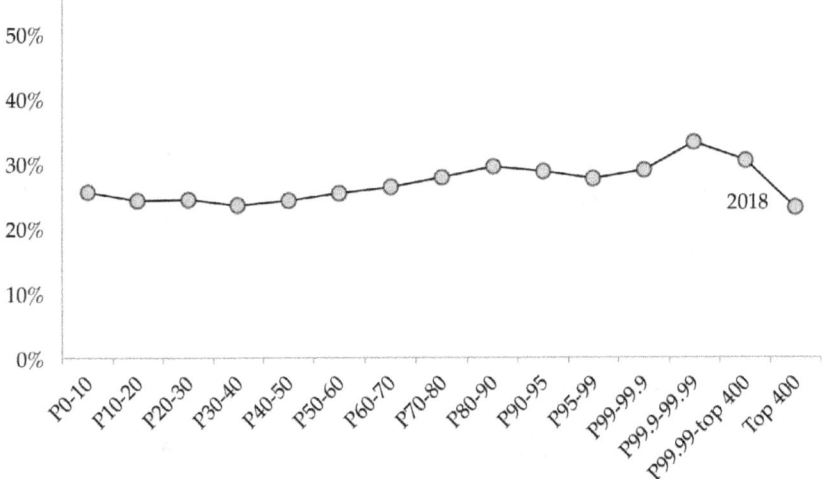

Average Tax Rates (all taxes, divided by income) by Income Groups.
Saez, Zucman "Progressive Wealth Taxation" (2019)

some one person or group of persons always will have dominating coercive power, and since that power creates and protects private property, the dominant person has incentive to use that power.

Not uncommonly in the nation-states, state security forces (military and police) will dominate, yet the security forces pledge loyalty, cede decision authority, and convey effective coercive power to a monarch, a dictator, a president, a prime minister or a parliament. In the case of "military Government" or martial law, the senior officer of the security forces decides the use of the dominant coercive power. Even in a region that has large, wealthy, well-established institutions of government, a gang, or militia may be the effective government, the dominant coercive force, in a neighborhood or subregion.

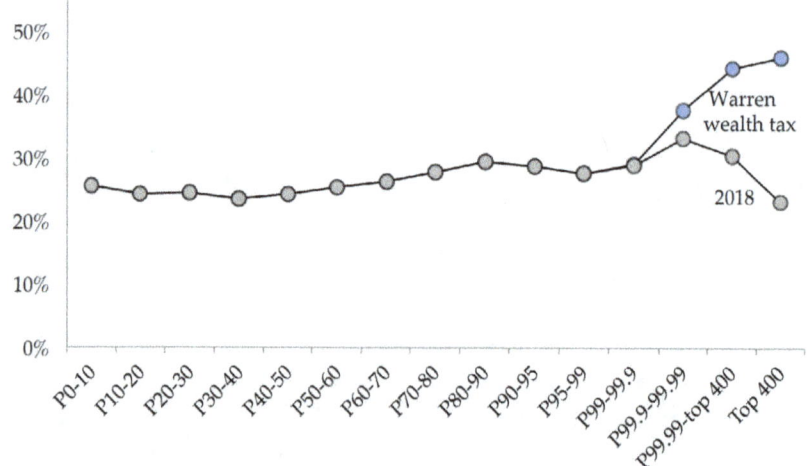

Average Tax Rates (all taxes, divided by income) by Income Groups.
Saez, Zucman "Progressive Wealth Taxation" (2019)

Sometimes the region of a nation-state will have no powerful force that exercises authority throughout its territory. The militias of contending warlords or gang members divide the exercise of coercive power among themselves, such as Afghanistan at the times of the Soviet and American invasions, and Somalia at the time of the American invasion, and northern Europe during the era of the Roman Empire. American and European critics of such regimes sometimes call them "failed states," a condescending term used to justify invading the failed state.

Gross Domestic Product or GDP – When a news announcer in our modern enlightened age mentions the "Economy," they most often refer to GDP. Economists often speak of GDP as the fundamental measure of social wellbeing. GDP is GNI Gross National Income plus or minus some relatively minor other stuff. GNI is the sum of all the incomes in a national subset of the Society.

To get GDP, we can start with GNI, add the depreciation of capital equipment (usually about 16% of GDP in the US), plus all the stuff sold to foreigners, minus all the stuff bought from foreigners (foreign transactions net about +/- 2% of GDP for large modern countries).

Since the Ten Percent own more than two-thirds of the depreciating capital, the Aristocracy has a bit larger share of GDP than of GNI. Typically, all the news announcer knows about GDP is whether GDP is larger this quarter than the previous quarter (interpreted as good news) or smaller (interpreted as bad news).

The Professors perform many versions of the perennial hit *Growth of GDP*. The Old One Adam Smith wrote the Tale of the Invisible Hand distributing income more or less evenly among the people, though he knew that Workers' incomes were so small and unsteady that Workers sickened and starved during business cycles.

In our modern enlightened era in the US, the income of the Aristocracy is about 20% of GDP, the income of the Nine Percent is about 30% of GDP, and the income of the 90 Percent is about 50% of GDP.

"... the top 10% income share is 50.5% in 2018..... The top 1% income share increased from 20.7% in 2016 to 22.0% in 2017 and remained stable at 22.0% in 2018."

– Emmanuel Saez, February 2020

See the chapters **"Growth and Income Disparity"** and **"Corporations, the Free Market, and the Invisible Hand."**

Income Stratum	Portion of GNI & GDP
Ninety Percent	50%
Nine Percent	30%
Aristocracy	20%

Growth – Usually implying growth of GDP. (Coincidentally, one of the most frequently performed stories of the Professors is *Growth of GDP*). You may often hear the word "Growth" used as though it were a synonym of "Prosperity," but it isn't.

See **Prosperity**.

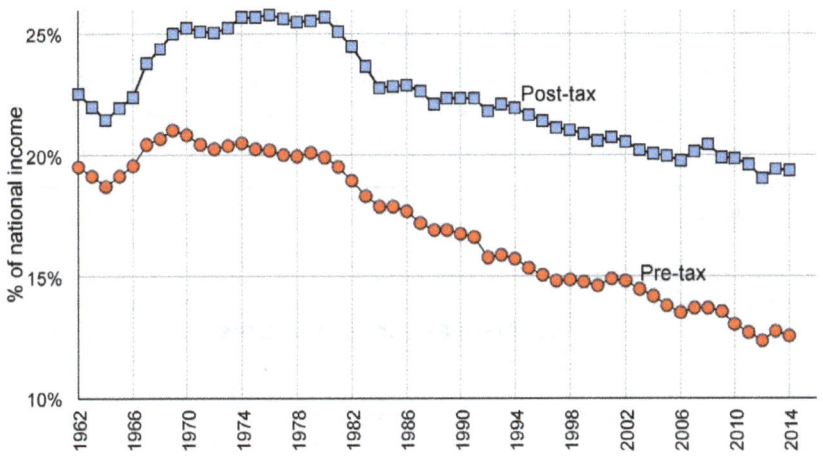

Source: Appendix Tables II-B1 and II-C1
United States income shares.
Graph: Saez, Piketty, and Zucman (Dec 2016)

Growth of Real Incomes – Per the United States Census Bureau, household income in the United States in constant 2018 dollars was

Real Household Income in United States			
Percentile	1967	2018	Increase
50th	$47,085	$63,179	34%
90th	$99,141	$184,292	86%
95th	$125,244	$248,728	98%

(constant 2018 dollars)

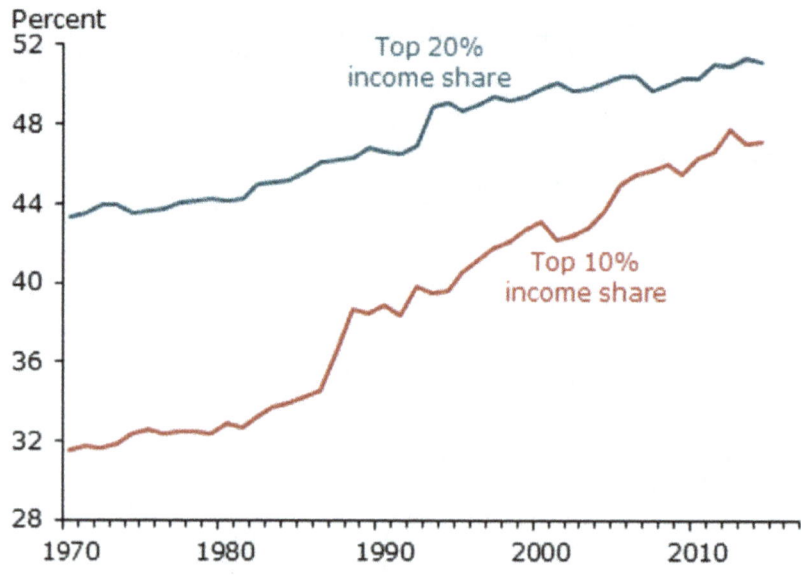

US Before Tax Income Shares

Source: Census Bureau (Table H-2), World Top Incomes database
Graph: Lansing and Markiewicz, "Consequences of Rising Income Inequality" (2016)

Income Disparity – a.k.a. Income Inequality, describes large differences in incomes between the wealthiest people in the Society and the least wealthy people. The existence of dramatic Income Disparity corresponds with undemocratic dominance of the Government by the Aristocracy.

Income – *See* **Growth of Real Income**

Income Inequality – *See* **Income Disparity.**

Inequality – *See* **Income Disparity.**

Ingenious Innovative Job Creators – A term in TOC generally applied to employers. But also, when the Staffs seek tax reductions for their clients, the Aristocrats, they portray the Aristocrats as Ingenious Innovative Job Creators. In any case, the goal of reducing taxes almost always motivates those who use the term. Ingenious Innovative Job Creators need not be ingenious, nor innovative, nor need they create jobs.

It's not obvious that an employer creates a condition of work to be done, rather than recognizing a pre-existing condition, perhaps one which a Worker has pointed out. In the case of the Aristocrat whose Staff seeks a tailored paragraph in the tax law, the Aristocrat may well have no awareness of the condition, and no particular such condition (of work to be done) need exist. If a Capitalist hires a Worker, then the Worker merits the glory of recognition as a "Job Creator" equally as might the Capitalist, but neither very obviously so.

Janissary Recruitment in the Balkans

In our modern enlightened era, "Job Creator" is a term of art among lobbyists seeking tax reductions from legislators. There was earlier use of "job creation" and related terms, but generally they referred to government policy or social behaviors affecting thousands and millions of people and not to individuals (such as owners of factories) and their actions.

In 1993, Joseph Ritter reported on research showing that job creation occurs relatively steadily over time, while "job destruction" occurs rapidly in seasonal or business cycle downturns. He also noted that job creation is nearly the same thing as "job finding," and job destruction is the same as "job separation." He affirmed job creation as a social activity, a market process, and seems to have been the first to have defined job creation as an act of firms. Ritter wrote, "Gross flows — the creation and destruction of specific jobs or the movement of workers into and out of employment — are the immediate outcomes of labor market processes. When a firm closes a plant, it destroys jobs. When it opens a plant, it creates jobs."

In an interesting 1987 article, Ake Blomqvist discussed job creation as a possible government policy. Interestingly, he described job creation for graduates of universities in less developed countries (the scope of the paper) as counterproductive if the students receive subsidies (grants and loans), but that's another story.

Richard Greene, in a 1982 article summarizing the state of research in "job generation," noted Birch's study and others. Incidentally, he observed, "Differences in net employment growth are largely the result of differences in the rates at which job losses are replaced, varying greatly from area to area."

In a 1981 article, *Who creates jobs?* David L. Birch wrote of developing a data source that facilitated the economic modeling of job creation as an activity of Firms, and an objective of government policies. In this context, he found that about 2/3 of all net additional jobs occurred in small (fewer than 20 employees) Firms, though not all small Firms. He wrote, "The job creators are the relatively few younger ones that start up and expand rapidly in their youth, outgrowing the "small" designation in the process."

Workers, as the Old One Adam Smith knew, were often the first to recognize productive improvements, so the modifier "Ingenious Innovative" almost always properly applies to them, not to their employer. The Old Ones never mentioned "job creators" or "job creation" or "create jobs." Nor did Ayn Rand. In TOC, the Workers are never called Job Creators, a term reserved only for Capitalists possessing large amounts of money. Like employers, Workers don't create jobs either, since a job requires at least one person who buys labor and at least one person who sells labor. That is, unless a robot replaces one of the persons, but that's another story.

The term "Job Creator," as a reference to individuals, is a neologism, nearly unknown before 2005, per Google Ngram (books.google.com/ngrams). Before that, use of the term "job creation" almost always referred to social behaviors, government policies and market processes (Birch, 1981; Greene, 1982; Blonqvist, 1987; Ritter, 1993). "Job Creator," in our modern enlightened era, is a term coined in the process of persuading a legislator to reduce income taxes for employers. Thus, the modern term "Job Creator" is an absurdity.

In principle, a government can hire people as civil service or military personnel, even if the government has no intention to apply Labor to a task. In practice, governments have hired people during periods of severe unemployment. In the US, to avoid political embarrassment, the political leadership must identify something "useful" for these people to do, like paint murals or build trails in national parks, for examples. More often, when politicians promise to "create jobs," they refer to changes in regulations, loans or grants to businesses, other manipulations of policies and expenditures or tax reductions.

In the private sector, persons who make a tangible product engage in a transaction (or trade) in the market with the persons who buy the product. Jobs arise from such transactions.

All employers hire people, and some may exhibit ingenuity, but those characteristics don't clearly justify reducing employers' taxes.

See the chapter **The Buyer of Labor and the Nine Percent.**

Intellectual Property or IP – A government grant, to a person or Firm, of an exclusive monopoly on the use of an idea. The right to use may be rented (via "royalties") or sold to others by the owner of the Intellectual Property. Ostensibly, IP compensates artists and scientists for bringing new ideas into the world. However, IP disincentivizes use of the idea, discourages new ideas that the idea may inspire, creates both a kind of property and a group of bad people (the violators of the property), contributes to monopoly practices, and establishes an industry of lawyers and accountants who challenge or defend IP in court and oversee the collection of royalties. Manifestly, IP isn't necessary for the production of new ideas, although it can hobble discovery or effective use of some ideas. Economist Joseph Stiglitz (2013, ch.2) writes that America's IP laws inhibit innovation and, by design, maximize monopoly rents (profits exceeding competitive profits). Provided they have sufficient equipment and materials for their work, sufficient income for the prosperity of their families and recognition for their works, artists and scientists bring new ideas into the world without resort to IP to which they may be entitled by law.

Invisible Hand – An articulation by Adam Smith of the notion that an individual, by pursuing their own interest, does thereby improve the Society. The phrase is usually taken out of context from a subtopic of a discussion of domestic versus foreign trade in Smith's book *The Theory of Moral Sentiments* (1759, p.128), which Smith used again in his *Wealth of Nations* (1776, p.242). That context sprawls across several paragraphs, which we abbreviate here, in Smith's words:

> *But it is only for the sake of profit that any man employs a capital in the support of industry; ... He generally, indeed, neither intends to promote the public interest, nor knows how much he is promoting it. ... he intends only his own security; ... he intends only his own gain; and he is in this, as in many other cases, led by an invisible hand to promote an end which was no part of*

his intention. Nor is it always the worse for the society that it was no part of it. By pursuing his own interest, he frequently promotes that of the society more effectually than when he really intends to promote it.

Labor – As often seen in the TOC (Tale of Capitalism), a word will have two meanings. "Labor" and "Worker" are close synonyms. Also, Labor is the productive activity of the Workers. In the sense of activity, Labor transforms Capital into valuable and useful products. The wage, the cost of Labor, is the cost sufficient to get a Worker to show up for work next week (Smith, 1776, ch.VIII; Kelly, 2003, ch.1; Marx & Engels, 1848, p.8; Ricardo, 1821, ch.V) and relates rarely and temporarily and secondarily to the value of the products. See Workers.

Labor Theory of Value – One of the Tales of the Old One Ricardo. "In estimating the exchangeable value of stockings, for example, we shall find that their value, comparatively with other things, depends on the total quantity of labour necessary to manufacture them, and bring them to market." (Ricardo, 1821, ch.I)

Land – The Old Ones Adam Smith and, especially, David Ricardo, wrote of three indispensable factors of production: Labor, Capital, and Land. Ricardo gave attention to the Rent a landlord can collect from their agricultural Land, which amount is determined by the value of crops grown on the land of poorest quality. If the poorest tilled land produces 10 tons per season per acre of tomatoes, then the value of those tomatoes is the cost of Labor to produce them, which is the cost of feeding the Labor sufficiently that they will show up for work during the next week, and the Rent available from this poorest Land is nothing but a token ceremonial fee to acknowledge permission to farm and ownership. If the next poorest land produces 20 tons per season per acre of tomatoes with the same Labor of cultivation, then the Rent on this next poorest Land is equal to zero (the value of the Rent on the poorest Land), plus the value of the additional production of 10 tons of tomatoes. If the best Land produces 50 tons per season per acre of tomatoes with the same Labor of cultivation as the poorest Land, then the Rent on the best Land is equal to the value of 40 tons of tomatoes. The Professors performed variations of Ricardo's Tales of the value of Labor and the value of Rents on Land. They remain key Tales of economics with numerous analogs in realms of thought far removed from agricultural Land, such as the value of obsolete computer equipment and Supercompensation of CEOs, even in our enlightened modern era.

See **Wealth** *for an example involving a theme park, a hotel, and an orange grove.*

Managers – Managers oversee the planning and operation of Firms and the direction of workers. Owners may also Manage, if they wish, but Ownership doesn't require it. The notion of Management originated early in the period of the great wars. From then until our enlightened modern era, four types of Managers have evolved: Supervisors (a.k.a. Managers), Directors, Executives, and the Chief Executive Officer (CEO).

Marginal Tax Rate – In our enlightened modern era, we have graduated income taxes, a.k.a. progressive income taxes. Smith (1776, Bk.V, pt.2) and Marx & Engels (1848) both mentioned this method in which a person with small income pays a small proportion of their personal income for the tax, and a person with large income pays a large portion.

In the evolution of our modern tax systems, various schemes have been tried for interpreting "small" and "large" and tables describing tax due at various levels (or brackets) of small, intermediate, and large incomes.

The marginal tax rate is the proportion of tax which the taxpayer must pay on the next dollar of income they get. Thus, the top marginal tax rate is the tax that will apply to the next dollar of income received by persons of greatest income if they receive more income. For example, if the tax rates on the first $100,000 and the next $100,000 are 10% and 20%, respectively, and the tax rate on income exceeding $200,000 is 30%, then a person with income of $175,000 will pay tax of $10,000 on the first $100,000, and tax of $15,000 on the $75,000, for a total tax of $25,000. This taxpayer's marginal rate is 20%, which is the rate that will apply to the 175,001st dollar of income if and when received. If the taxpayer gets $200,000 of income, then the tax will be 10% of the first $100,000, and 20% of the second $100,000, for a total of $30,000. However, the marginal tax rate will be 30%

because that is the rate that will apply to the 200,001st dollar of income. In our enlightened modern era, the largest incomes vastly exceed the top bracket, so the top marginal tax rate is very nearly the rate that applies to the largest incomes.

Marx, Karl – Marx and his collaborator Friedrich Engels are two of the Old Ones. Their *Communist Manifesto,* which they wrote in 1848 on behalf of the Communist League (an organization that disbanded in 1852), clearly called for abolition of private property and overthrow of existing government, and less prominently advocated a graduated income tax, abolition of child labor and free education in public schools.

The *Manifesto* appeared in dozens of languages throughout the world. In the *Manifesto*, they described in detail, and with scorn, what they called the "capitalist system" in their immensely influential economic treatise *Das Kapital* (a.k.a. *Capital*,1867). Marx taught that the economic system of a society (the means of production) determines the political character of the society, an idea prominent in modern understanding of history and politics. Like many others zealous for their causes, Marx imagined that communist revolution was scientific and inevitable.

In our enlightened modern age, we often attribute Marx's ideas and the books *Manifesto* and *Capital* to Marx alone, although we would more accurately attribute them to Marx & Engels, because Engels contributed heavily and indispensably in all these regards.

Marx lived and died in near poverty, sustained by subsidies from Engels. His remains lie in a cemetery in Highgate, London, UK.

Minimum Subsistence – *See* **Subsistence.**

Monop – A Monop is a Monopoly or Monopsony, depending on context.

See **Monopoly.** *See* **Monopsony.**

Monopoly – A general economic condition in which buyers have no choice of sellers but must buy from a single seller. In pure form, which seldom persists for long without government controls, there is exactly one seller.

In otherwise competitive markets, if there are fewer than seven sellers, then usually, the economic effect is so similar to that of a pure Monopoly that we often consider each of the sellers, in practice, a Monopoly. Or, if one seller sells more than 30% of the product in a market, then usually that seller is, effectively, a Monopoly. If there is a Monopoly in some product or service, then no fair trade can exist because a buyer gets no change in the value of trade by choosing another seller.

See **Monop.**

See **Monopsony.**

John D. Rockefeller (ca. 1875)

Monopsony – A general economic condition in which sellers have no choice of buyers but must sell to a single buyer. In pure form, which seldom persists for long without government controls, there is exactly one buyer. In otherwise competitive markets, if there are fewer than seven buyers, then usually, the economic effect is so similar to that of a pure Monopsony that we often consider each of the buyers, in practice, a Monopsony. Or, if one buyer buys more than 30% of the product in a market, then usually that buyer is, effectively, a Monopsony. If there is a Monopsony in some product or service, then no fair trade can exist because a seller gets no change in the value of trade by choosing another buyer.

See **Monop.** *See* **Monopoly.**

Nine Percent – The Nine Percent and the Aristocracy, considered together, are the Ten Percent of households that have larger incomes and greater wealth than anyone else in the Society. In the US, the Nine Percent get roughly 30% of national aggregate household incomes. About 40% of their incomes arises from ownership of Capital and businesses, and most of their income arises from their Labor.

90 Percent – The least wealthy 90% of the Society, that is, all of the Society except the Ten Percent. The 90 Percent includes most of the Workers and small business owners and all the poor people. Nearly all their income arises from their Labor.

Wealth Shares of Bottom 90% and Top 0.1% Families

The figure depicts the share of total household wealth owned by bottom 90% and top 0.1% obtained by capitalizing income tax returns (Saez and Zucman 2016). The unit of analysis is the family.

99 Percent – All the Society except the Aristocracy, that is, the 90 Percent and the Nine Percent, combined.

Occupy Wall Street – A protest movement that began on September 17, 2011, in Zuccotti Park in New York City and spread from there throughout the world. OWS had no formal leadership and no clear agenda. The Wikipedia article attributes predecessor protests at the University of California in 2008, and Kalle Lasn of the Canadian group "Adbusters" as the initiator of the call for protest in New York. Extreme inequalities of wealth and incomes, greed, unfair influence of large corporations, and corruption in government were principal concerns. Observers of OWS often heard the slogan, "We are the 99%."

Old Ones – The Old Ones wrote the most significant early Tales, in both small and immense volumes, for which understanding requires careful study. The Old Ones were Adam Smith, David Ricardo, Karl Marx, and Friedrich Engels.

One Percent – *See* **Aristocracy.**

Overall Income – Ordinary or customary income, combined with all other increases in wealth, without exception.

OWS – *See* **Occupy Wall Street.**

Piketty, Thomas – An Economist of our enlightened modern age and author of the intensively researched book *Capital in the Twenty-First Century* and the subsequent *Capital and Ideology*. Dr. Piketty's writings provide detailed information on the inequality of incomes and wealth from times before the Old Ones to the present.

Political Capitalist – *See* **Socialism** and **Downward Trickle.**

Political Economy – a term used sometimes to refer to the mutual influence of the government and the economy, and the pertinent range of decisions.

Potential Conflict of Interest – *An actual conflict of interest.* – Jason Zweig, 2015

Price – In a trade or exchange, one trader offers some items to another trader who offers other items in exchange. We assume that each trader offers a collection of items, with the items in each collection practically equal to all other items in that collection. The "price" is the number of items in the first trader's offer divided by the number of items in the other trader's offer. When the grocer offers tomatoes to a customer in exchange for money, the price might be expressed as dollars per pound. If the customer takes 2.5 pounds of tomatoes from the grocer and pays $9.48, then the price is $9.48/2.5 = $3.79 per pound.

Professors – *See* **Business School Professors.**

Prosperity – Thriving with comforts and happiness. Not a synonym for "Growth."
See **Growth.**

Put – An option to sell shares of a stock at a stated strike price before a stated expiration date. If you write a Put, then you agree to buy the stock at the strike price. If the current price of the stock drops below the strike price of the Put, then the Put increases in value.

Warning: if you venture into buying and selling Puts or Calls for the first time, then keep your trades very small and few to avoid losing a lot of money.
See **Call.**

Rand, Ayn – Rand escaped from Stalinist Russia and took refuge in New York City, where she established an anti-communist intellectual salon. She advocated for the idea that virtuous selfishness is objective and rational. She wrote a lucid defense of capitalism in her book *Virtue of Selfishness* (1961). Her books remain widely read in our modern enlightened era, including *Fountainhead, Atlas Shrugged,* and others.

Real Incomes – *See* **Growth of Real Incomes.**

Rent – *See* **Land.**

Ricardo, David – The Old One Ricardo acquired wealth trading shares on the Exchange. He wrote the treatise *On the Principles of Political Economy and Taxation* (1821), expostulating precise and enduring economic theories. Among these was the profound, but hardly obvious, Tale of Comparative Advantage, in which he showed that two countries, with their Workers unable to travel between them, could maximize their aggregate incomes if each concentrated their Workers' efforts on making those products that they were best able to produce, selling what excess they couldn't use to inhabitants of the other country. Robert Barro, an economist of our modern enlightened era, reminds us of the Tale of Ricardian Equivalence, named for its originator, which implies that a stimulative government subsidy doesn't stimulate because the people save the money received instead of spending it, which more or less describes the behavior of the Aristocracy, the usual recipients. Ricardo also explained that the natural level of Workers' wages is the price that enables the Workers to subsist.

Sachs, Jeffrey – A Professor and a relatively intelligible Economist of our enlightened modern era. Dr. Sachs advocates collaborative relationships between governments and privately owned organizations. During the late 1900s, Sachs advised new governments, including the government of Russia, that emerged when the Soviet Union ended. He advises the Secretary-General of the United Nations.

Saez, Emmanuel – A research Economist, Director of the Center for Equitable Growth at the University of California in Berkeley and a collaborator with Piketty, Stantcheva, and Zucman, among others. Economists hold Saez in high regard for expressing his views well and for the mathematical underpinnings that support them. Saez frequently uses easily understandable graphics, uncommon among Economists.

Seller – See **Buyer**.

Shareholders – *See* **Corporation**.
    Synonym: **Stockholders**.

Smith, Adam – The earliest of the four Old Ones. Often remembered for his Tale of the Invisible Hand (*Sentiments* [1759], *Wealth* [1776]). Smith also articulated the principles of the division of labor and of enhancements of wealth through technological innovation. Some Political Capitalists may be heard to assert that Smith was a Political Capitalist, which he was not. However, Smith described the economic system of his time, which was in his day generally accepted as the only economic system, a natural condition, and the default condition if the state protects private property and doesn't participate in distributing wealth or income. Smith wrote that workers compete, bidding against one another for employment, which competition keeps their wages to a "scanty subsistence."

Socialism – An amorphous social and political movement, historically manifested in various forms, clustered around the concept that all persons have the right to a sustaining share of the political participation and economic benefits of the general Society.

Socialism has no primary leader who articulates the principles and beliefs of Socialism. An early organized form was Chartism in the 1800s, a rallying of Workers around the People's Charter of 1838, a list of six democratic political reforms, including universal male suffrage and secret ballots. Closely associated with labor unions, Chartists organized some of the earliest strikes of workers against their employers, seeking higher wages and improved working conditions among other things.

Early Socialism included benevolent organizations providing housing for workers and communally owned businesses. From Socialism emerged the concepts of universal public education, the graduated income tax and abolition of child labor.

The "Communist League" was an organized political splinter party that commissioned the Old Ones Engels and Marx to write the party's program in 1847, which was published as the *Manifesto of the Communist Party* in 1848. The League was formally dissolved by the remaining members in 1852. Nearly all members of the Communist League would have regarded themselves as Socialists.

Twentieth century autocrats, including Stalin, Mao, and some autocrats of our enlightened modern era, have called themselves Communists. Some Political Capitalists assert with invalid inference that Socialism is or leads to autocracy. Stalin was an autocrat, Stalin was a Communist, Communists are Socialists, so Socialists are autocrats, so they reason, which is the Capitalist's Fallacy.

Society – All of the people – the Aristocrats, the Nine Percent, the 90 Percent – everyone. The Society organized itself into groups called Firms to find, gather, produce, and distribute stuff.

Sound Dues – A toll payment exacted by the King of Denmark on merchant vessels passing through the Oresund and the Denmark Straits, the only marine passages between the North Sea and the Baltic Sea. Any list of grand Monops would include the Sound Dues. The King required the master of the vessel to present a manifest showing the estimated value of the ship's contents and hull to the King's officer and pay the toll of about one-half to three percent, except that if the officer judged the master's estimates were too low, then the officer could pay the master the stated value on the manifest and take possession. King Eric built the Krogen fortress at Elsinore in the early 1400s with which he enforced the toll in earnest from 1429 (Wikipedia). The Sound Dues had existed in some form as early as 1319 or perhaps earlier (Hessenland, 1855), and were discontinued by treaty in 1857.

Staff – The existence and work of the Staffs isn't widely publicized. What we know of them consists of a bit of fact and substantial portions of rumor and surmise.

Aristocrats and their families often have Staffs. (Note: Staffs is the plural of Staff. In general, one Aristocrat has one Staff, two Aristocrats have two Staffs.) Anyone can have a Staff, and sensibly so, if a specialist astutely managing the money can produce sufficient income that a small fraction of the income will pay the specialist's salary.

A Staff is one or more people, including accountants, lawyers, financial experts, lobbyists, administrators, and others, who supervise the household finances and the owned businesses of the Aristocrats. The distinction between Managers of owned companies and the Staff may blur in practice. Staffs report regularly to their principals on the change in value of the principals' wealth (which includes the positive and negative effects of after-tax income) during the latest quarter ended, and they hope always to be able to report some increase in overall income from the prior period. The Aristocrat may know little about managing money or running a business, but they tend to understand the significance of increasing or decreasing wealth. Staffers who report that the Aristocrat's wealth increased reliably from quarter to quarter will likely enjoy increases in their

The Denmark Staff. (Maersk Lines, 1914)

own wealth. Staffers who report overall income declining from quarter to quarter may not remain in the employ of the Aristocrat the following year.

The 90 Percent and most of the Nine Percent, almost always having no Staffs, can make but amateurish efforts to increase their own wealth.

Staffers always seek to reduce their employer's tax burden because reduced taxes increase an Aristocrat's after-tax income, and positive after-tax income increases the Aristocrat's total wealth. They seek to modify government regulations to improve their Aristocrat's businesses. Regulations can provide or obstruct opportunities to profit in many ways, these among them:

1. by increasing the businesses' revenues,

2. by adjusting constraints on competition,

3. by providing an opportunity to supply the government with goods or services,

4. by clarifications of definitions of taxable income,

5. by prudently decreasing the incomes of suppliers, workers, customers or competitors or

6. by making available or denying access to a public resource.

Staffers of different Aristocrats may discover commonality of interests on some matters and collaborate to increase their Aristocrats' overall incomes. The aggregate efforts, blameless of any immorality or significant violations of law, of all the Staffs of all the Aristocrats maintain and intensify the inequality of incomes in the Society. As though moved by an Invisible Hand, the Staffs produce inequality of incomes.

Stiglitz, Joseph – After the great wars, the Economist Dr. Joseph Stiglitz received high awards and wrote widely read books on asymmetrical information (where parties to a trade have differing knowledge of the character of the goods exchanged) and on the economic costs of extreme inequality of incomes.

Stockholders – *See* **Shareholders.**

Stockholders – *See* **Shareholders.**

Subsistence, Subsistence Minimum – The Old Ones referred to a level of wealth or income called "subsistence" as representing the lowest price an employer could expect to pay for Labor for any significant period of time, and they were in agreement that this was the approximate lower bound of wage that Labor would fetch in the Free Market for any extended period of time.

Veblen (1899, p.73) gives the most precise definition of Subsistence:

The subsistence minimum is of course not a rigidly determined allowance of goods, definite and invariable in kind and quantity; but for the purpose in hand it may be taken to comprise a certain, more or less definite, aggregate of consumption required for the maintenance of life.

What essentials life requires will differ from individual to individual, and they differ according to the sensibilities and practicalities of different societies in different places. For example, in our enlightened modern age, in a large European city, the Society might judge indoor plumbing necessary for subsistence, as the lack of it might threaten public health, even though indoor plumbing may have been rare in the same city 300 years ago.

Engels (1848) saw subsistence as the lower limit of wages, which results from the competition of workers with each other:

To this competition of the worker there is but one limit; no worker will work for less than he needs to subsist.

If he must starve, he will prefer to starve in idleness rather in toil. True, this limit is relative; one needs more than another, one is accustomed to more comfort than another; ...

Supercompensation – Money that Firms pay to their CEOs far in excess of the money paid to other employees of the Firm, far in excess of the value they produce for the company and far in excess of the value of a human life. Supercompensation first appeared during the time of Reagan. Per Piketty (2017), the declines in the highest marginal income tax rates in the United States and Britain since 1980 allowed CEOs to collect Rents. During the period of relatively high tax rates, the CEO would get only a fourth or less of each additional dollar of income. The CEO plausibly considered it not worth significant effort to argue for a raise larger than what the Board of Directors offered, and that he would better spend his time tuning the company to increase the unrealized gain on the shares he held. After the tax cuts in the 1980s and later years, large increases in his own pay became worth the CEO's effort to procure, the effect on the CEO's after-tax income having become significant. In our enlightened modern era, not infrequently, the CEO (or other highly compensated employee) will receive pay more than 150 times the value of the median amount of money paid to individual employees. At this writing, $15 million per year is ordinary compensation for an executive in a publicly traded corporation. In the United States, if the typical

Worker does excellent work every year and so earns substantial pay raises every year for 50 years, then the Worker will have approximately the same level of pay as the typical CEO has today.

Supervisors – Managers who manage Workers directly.

Tales – *See* **Old Ones.**

Tea Party – An old political party for Political Capitalists. For hundreds of years, the party has pursued the primary policy objective of increasing the wealth (including the after-tax income) of the Aristocracy during the next two or three years. All other policies are subordinate, less important, reversible should they become inconvenient and generally advocated or promoted or opposed or ignored at one time or another for expediency. Since the policies of the Tea Party generally don't conflict with and are consistent with their professional interests, most of the Staffs prefer the Tea Party. Aristocrats don't necessarily prefer the Tea Party. The Tea Party, also called at times the GOP and the Trump Party, flourished during the time of Reagan, then faded, then continued to fluctuate in popularity every few years, and it persists in our enlightened era. See also Curve of Laffer.

Ten Percent – The wealthiest tenth of the population of the Society. The Old Ones Marx and Engels called this tenth the Bourgeoisie and referred to them as the owners of Capital.

TOC – The Tale of Capitalism.

Trade – In a trade, there is always at least one buyer and one seller. These are the parties to the trade. Each of the parties gives up something they want less in exchange for something they want more. Each party benefits from the trade. The benefit is the difference between the thing wanted more and the thing wanted less, a kind of profit for each party. Each party has a choice whether to participate in the trade. Each party may decline to participate. Each party may choose some other person with whom to trade. Usually, the buyer is the party who gives up cash, and the seller is the other party. If both parties have a wide range of counterparties from whom to choose, and if they both participate freely, without coercion or deception or special privilege or special incapacity, then we call it a fair trade.

Transaction – *Synonym of* **Trade.**

Unemployment – The Old One Engels noted in his *Condition of the Working Class in England* (1845) that the factories would build up their operation, sometimes to a fast tempo, and continue producing for six to ten years. Then a waning of revenues would affect most of them more or less simultaneously so that the product of a factory working at capacity couldn't be sold at a price sufficient to pay the costs of operation. Among these costs was the wages of the workers since the workers weren't considered legally interested in the ownership and profits. Simply reducing the wages did not go well with the workers. For the better paid workers, their pride suffered, and they felt unjustly rewarded for their efforts, kindling resentments and animosity. But for most workers, since their wages just barely sufficed to feed their families for a few more days, a reduction in wages implied insufficient food to sustain them, and some of them would become desperate and unpredictable. The level of wages, like all other choices in the Firm, were the decision of the managers, the executives, the board of directors, the Staffs, the Ingenious Innovative Job Creators and ultimately the Owners. Given the adverse effects of reducing wages, the Ingenious Innovative Job Creators typically chose to dismiss some of the Workers so that the number of remaining Workers corresponded with the level of production. "Dismiss" meant discontinuing the employment and the wages. The people of the general Society described the dismissed Worker as "unemployed" and existing in a state of "unemployment." Veblen (1899) refers to the unemployed as the "underfed class." Since multiple factories in the region would dismiss Workers at about the same time, the Workers contended with each other for jobs. Few Workers could quickly find a new job and a new stream of wages. Since they didn't participate in the profits of the Firms, and since their wages had dropped to zero, "unemployment" could mean "starvation" (Smith, 1776, ch.VIII).

Wealth – Roughly synonymous with the noun "riches," or in the adjective form "Wealthy," synonymous with "rich," Wealth has multiple meanings in the Tale of Capitalism.

Most often, Wealth refers to a kind of property capable of becoming the Capital component in the transformation of Capital by Labor into product exchanged for incrementally larger Capital for the owner. More than half the income of the Aristocracy consists of the increments this kind of Wealth produces. Another use of Wealth, usually in the adjective form Wealthy, pertains to a person with a relatively large overall income, especially when that income is Supercompensation.

Wealth and income are closely related in the sense that Wealth is Capital that produces a surplus or profit or income net of costs. We can think of the value of Capital, in terms of Wealth, as the income we expect it to produce in the future. Thus, if an asset produces $5,000 per year, and if we expect it to produce 5% (more or less) of its value each year, then the asset has a value of $100,000. If a change in taxation or inflation reduces the annual production of value to $4,500 per year, a 10% decline, then we expect the value of the asset to decline 10% also, to $90,000. If the asset is an orange grove and a corporation constructs a grand theme park on adjacent land, then the value of the orange grove may increase immensely, since it would become the most favorable site of a grand hotel with 100 splendidly appointed rooms producing after-tax income net of expenses of $10,000/room/year or $1 million/year total, which would have a value of $20 million if we expect 5% of value per year, and from this increase in Rents (See Rent), the owner of the orange grove would have an increase in asset value of $19.9 million.

The Aristocracy are always considered Wealthy. Not uncommonly, the Ten Percent are considered Wealthy, depending on the context. The 90 Percent are never considered Wealthy. The Economists Chetty and Hendren (2014, 2018) found that children of households in less wealthy neighborhoods that move to wealthier neighborhoods become wealthier adults than children of households in less wealthy neighborhoods that don't move.

Workers – People for whom most of their income, and nearly the entire income of most Workers, arises from compensation for their Labor. Labor is the productive activity of the Workers. Nearly all of the 90 Percent are Workers or dependents of Workers. Most of the Ten Percent are Workers, too, though they tend to derive relatively more income from their property.

Albert Parsons, leader of a railway strike in 1877

See **Wealth.** *See* **Labor.**

Working Class – A loose term, generally all the Society except the Ten Percent. See Workers

Afterword

*Chance plays an important role in life,
and you can decide to be bitter about it
or you can decide to understand
that success is not entirely due to one's own efforts,
and neither is failure.*

– Chief Justice John Roberts

The *Tale of Capitalism* isn't a polemic, but it shows our economic system results in a small number of people having wealth beyond dreams, and a large number of people in a scanty existence, with millions underfed. What can we do?

"Cassim in the Cave" by Maxfield Parrish. (1909).

What should we do? I prefer democracy, and in democracy we discuss ideas, then we decide. I offer the following as suggestions for discussion.

We can, if we choose, adjust our economic system a little (no grand revolution required) so that it preserves the productiveness of its incentives and disincentives, and so that it preserves and enhances the lives of the many who live in it.

The content of the preceding chapters suggests some of the things we can do, if we choose:

Distribution and Incentives. Neither Political Capitalism nor Political Socialism (1) distributes essential goods and services to all and (2) incentivizes the population to vigorous productivity. In countries around the world, people have tried the purest feasible forms of both. Political capitalism fails to fully distribute but tends to incentivize. Political socialism fails to incentivize but tends to distribute. Both have, in many cases, permitted dictatorial governments and corruption of public officials. We need not subject otherwise good ideas to purity tests to assure they are Capitalist enough or Socialist enough. Good ideas may be Capitalist or Socialist or neither or both. Let's allow criteria other than "Capitalism" and "Socialism" to guide our Society.

Meritocracy's limits. Consider the idea of meritocracy, the notion that some people deserve more and some people deserve less or none at all. We can keep meritocracy as part of the incentives, but not as the final determiner of who will fall asleep hungry tonight.

We need not presume that our central current problems result from the laziness, perfidy, foolishness, greed, or criminality of others. The structure and dynamic of our economic system imply that even if everyone had the innocent moral character of ideal Girl and Boy Scouts, the few with vast riches and the many with hunger would result.

In the US, government could provide every child, woman, and man, without exception, including prisoners and wealthy people, with $200 per month to spend as they wish, whether they merit it or not, at a cost of about $800 billion per year, financed by increasing the taxes on the Aristocracy. This would affirm by law and action that every person must have at least $2,400 per year of income to avoid the most brutal effects of poverty. Almost everyone would still want a job or business to provide a larger income for their families, so incentives and meritocracy would continue to inspire work. We could expect that most of the 90 Percent and nearly all of the 50 Percent would spend the monthly payment right away, rather than save much of it. The aggregate additional tax on the Aristocracy would closely approximate the aggregate payments, so aggregate money supply wouldn't change. But the trajectory and velocity of monetary circulation would change, so the central bank would monitor developments closely and act to prevent excessive inflation or deflation. The additional transactions generated by the people spending their monthly payments would generate jobs (though, with automation, robots might take some of those jobs). In the long term, the level of wages paid by employers would decline by the amount of the monthly payment, reducing the labor costs of the employer. Indexing the monthly payment amount to the per capita income of the Aristocracy would slow expanding income disparity.

Tax the rich. Government can tax incomes and Wealth progressively so that relatively larger incomes and accumulations of Wealth will bear relatively higher tax rates. Rand and other Political Capitalists predict that higher taxes cause Wealthy people to withdraw from financing productive businesses and having ideas; however, the historical record shows few occurrences. We might expect an income tax rate of 60% to 70% on larger incomes, and an annual property tax of around 1% on larger accumulations of Wealth. Tax rates at this level would likely slow or reverse expanding income and Wealth disparities and provide for essential and useful services of government. We can anticipate the Staffs of the Aristocrats will continue lawful efforts to weaken, reduce or prevent taxation of their client Aristocrats.

Competition. The regulated Free Market enables vigorous production and distribution. The regulation must prevent fraud and theft, and also, it must ensure competition. We haven't enough competition today, and we lack the full prosperity it would provide. If a Monop (a Monopoly or Monopsony) has more than 30% of the share of its market, then the regulator should divide it into two competitors of roughly equal size. If a Monop has fewer than 5 competitors, then the regulator should divide the largest competitor.

If no feasible competition can occur, as often seen with stock exchanges, public utilities, ports, public parks, schools, roads, and numerous other possibilities, then the regulator should diligently monitor and guide the Monop, or in rare cases the government should take it over and operate it. Intellectual property monopolies should be limited in duration. The government could apply a taxing system to intellectual properties similar to the Sound Dues taxation of vessels.

Distribution of the Surplus. We should reform the tradition of denying Labor a part of the surplus of sales less costs. Workers and Capitalists each take risks in business enterprises. Labor, materials, equipment and tools used in production have costs. Capital also has a cost, the rate of return that the Capitalist could expect from an alternate investment, a kind of calculation that Professors teach students in business schools. The owners and executives could announce this cost at the beginning of the year and collect this cost for the owners. Workers and owners could split profits that exceed the capital cost.

In my own view. Our current system doesn't distribute essential goods and services well. Both Capitalism and Socialism, and other sources as well, provide good ideas. Rewards for merit can provide incentive, but every person has essential economic necessities. Society can feasibly and usefully assure every person gets part of a subsistence minimum, whether they deserve it or not. Government can tax the wealthy at higher rates to moderate income and wealth inequalities. Free Markets function poorly without vigorous competition among buyers and sellers. Workers and owners can split the profits of business enterprises.

And one last thing. Ingenious Innovative Job Creators don't create jobs. Transactions – trades, that is – create jobs.

Thank you for reading my book. May you be happy and prosperous.

Images by Chapter

Initial Pages

The fall of the bottom 50% mirrors the rise of the top 1%, from Picketty, Saez, Zucman. (2016). *Distributional National Accounts: Methods and Estimates for the United States.*

1 **Onto This Stage**

Sign of the Third Base Tavern (photo by Daniel Brockman, 2016)

Decomposing the Top Decile, from Saez, Emmanuel. (June 30, 2016). *Striking it Richer.* (http://eml.berkeley.edu/~saez/saez-UStopincomes-2015.pdf).

2   **The 90 Percent**
    Bottom 90% wealth share, all methods, from Saez and Zucman. (2016). *Wealth Inequality in the United States since 1913 (The Quarterly Journal of Economics,* May 2016, http://eml.berkeley.edu/~saez/SaezZucman2016QJEAppendix.pdf).

3   **The Buyer of Labor and The Nine Percent**
    USA 2018 Wealth Shares and Pre-Tax Income Shares. Chart by Daniel Brockman.

4   **Workers, GDP, and Economists**
    US Before Tax Income Shares, from Lansing and Markiewicz (Oct 17, 2016).

5   **CEOs, Growth, and Prosperity of Society**
    GDP50 shrank during the 50 years ended 2014. Piketty, Saez and Zucman (Dec 2016)

6   **Supercompensation, Income, and The Exchange**
    Sculpture: *Solon* by Brenda Putnam. (1950). Architect of the Capitol (https://www.aoc.gov/explore-capitol-campus/art/solon-relief-portrait)

    Median Household Income in the United States, 2015 from United States Census Bureau. (Sep 2016). *Median Household Income in the United States: 2015.* (https://www.census.gov/library/visualizations/2016/comm/cb16-158_median_hh_income_map.html)

Examples of supercompensation in 2016. Chart by Daniel Brockman.

7   Land and Ricardo

Portrait of Ricardo by Thomas Phillips. (1821). National Portrait Gallery, UK. (https://en.wikipedia.org/wiki/David_Ricardo#/media/File:Portrait_of_David_Ricardo_by_Thomas_Phillips.jpg). While the National Portrait Gallery has claimed ownership of photographs of the portrait, itself a work of art in the public domain, the Intellectual Property Office cited in Nov 2015 the opinion of the European Court of Justice that rights may attach to original works, and not to photographs of original works. US law *(Bridgeman v. Corel,* 1999) is consistent with the European Court.

British shilling. (Wikimedia.org)

"Making Cloth". Textiles - *Man working at machines – Paterson, New Jersey* by Louis Hine. (1936-1937). National Research Project, NARA. (https://commons.wikimedia.org/wiki/File:Paterson,_New_Jersey_-_Textiles._(Man_working_at_machines.)_-_NARA_-_518626.jpg)

Comparative Advantage. Table by Daniel Brockman.

Killington Parish, UK Baptism Register (1820). Public Domain in US because all parties died more than 100 years ago.

8 Managers, Professors, and Engels

Friedrich Engels by William Hall (1879).

Samuel Compton's Spinning Mule (circa 1779), image by Pezzab (Wikimedia.org, Creative Commons Attribution-Share Alike license)

Sir Richard Arkwright 1732-1792, one of Lancashire's early capitalists. Portrait by Mather Brown (1790). (Wikipedia.org)

Thomas High's Spinning Jenny (circa 1764), published in Baines, Edward (1835), *History of the Cotton Manufacture in Great Britain* (Wikipedia.org).

9 The Eric Tetralogy: 1: Rents and Monops

Eric of Pomerania 1381-1459 (a.k.a. Eryk Pomorski. Muzeum: Zamek Ksiazat Pomorskich, Darlowo, Polska. Public domain photo image by Southerly Clubs of Stockholm, https://commons.wikimedia.org/wiki/File:Eryk_I_Pomorski_Dar%C5%82owo.jpg#/media/File:Eric_VII_the_Pomeranian_of_Denmark_(photo_2010).jpg)

Example Calculation of Landlord's Rent by Daniel Brockman.

10 The Eric Tetralogy: 2: The Tea Party

Boston Tea Party, by W.D. Cooper, *The History of North America* (1789, E. Newbury, London, https://en.wikipedia.org/wiki/Tea_Act#/media/File:Boston_Tea_Party-Cooper.jpg)

British East India Company Flag, listed "Flag of the British East India Company" from William Downman, *Notebook* (1685, https://commons.wikimedia.org/w/index.php?curid=4118976)

The Destruction of Tea at Boston Harbor, by Nathaniel Currier (1846, Public Domain, https://commons.wikimedia.org/wiki/File:Boston_Tea_Party_Currier_colored.jpg)

11 **The Eric Tetralogy: 3: The Firehose Up**
Oresund Map (1888) *(Karte des Öresund,* Quelle: Meyers Konversationslexikon von 1888, Band 10, Seite 61, Public Domain, https://commons.wikimedia.org/wiki/File:Karte_der_Umgebung_von_Kopenhagen.jpg)

Elizabeth I of England by George Gower, 1588, from Woburn Abbey, a.k.a. *Armada_Portrait* (National Portrait Gallery, Wikipedia, https://commons.wikimedia.org/wiki/File:Elizabeth_I_(Armada_Portrait).jpg)

12 **The Eric Tetralogy: 4: Ideas As Monops**
Coronation of Eric of Pomerania by Hans Peter Hansen (1884, Wikimedia.org, Public Domain, https://commons.wikimedia.org/wiki/File%3AErik_af_Pommern.jpg)

J. P. Morgan portrait (Wikipedia.org, Public Domain, https://en.wikipedia.org/wiki/J._P._Morgan)

13 Rand, Marx, and The Downward Trickle

Ayn Rand (1925, USSR passport photo, Public Domain, https://commons.wikimedia.org/wiki/File:Ayn_Rand.jpg)

Karl Marx (circa 1870) by John Jabez Edwin Mayall (UK National Portrait Gallery, http://www.npg.org.uk/collections/search/portrait/mw75680/Karl-Marx, Public Domain in USA, https://commons.wikimedia.org/wiki/File:Karl_Marx_by_Mayall_c1870.jpg)

Skyline of New York City (Mar 14, 1950, Gottscho-Schleisner, Inc., Library of Congress, LC-G613-56750, Public Domain, http://www.loc.gov/pictures/item/gsc1994001246/PP/)

Pyramids of Egypt – Sailors of USS Raleigh (ca. 1900, Library of Congress, http://www.loc.gov/pictures/item/det1994010117/PP/).

14 Corporations, The Free Market, and The Invisible Hand

James Lancaster VI (1596, National Maritime Museum, Greenwich, England, Public Domain, https://pt.wikipedia.org/wiki/Ficheiro:Jameslancaster.jpg)

East India Company Chop (1600s, The East India Company, Fair Use, https://www.theeastindiacompany.com/wp-content/uploads/2016/08/EIC-Chop.jpg)

"Certificate for Six shares of stock in a Corporation (1887)". *Chicago, Burlington & Quincy Railroad Stock Certificate.* (1887, Public Domain. https://commons.wikimedia.org/wiki/File:Chicago,_Burlington_%26_Quincy_Railroad_Stock_Certificate_1887.jpg)

"Market, Padua, Italy (1891)". *Palazzo della Ragione, Padua, Italy* (1891) by Paolo Salviati (1818-1894). (Hallwyl Museum, Public Domain, https://commons.wikimedia.org/wiki/File:Fotografi_fr%C3%A5n_Padua,_Sala_della_Ragione_-_Hallwylska_museet_-_102990.tif)

15 Capital and The Chairman

US Households by food security status, 2016, US Department of Agriculture, Economic Research Service. (Dec 2016). *Current Population Survey Food Security Supplement.*

16 The Old Ones and The 50 Percent

Adam Smith by John Kay (1790, Library of Congress, Public Domain, Wikimedia, https://commons.wikimedia.org/wiki/File:AdamSmith1790b.jpg)

17 Growth and Income Disparity

US GDP in billions of chained 2012 dollars, US Dept of Commerce, Bureau of Economic Analysis, bea.gov.

Top 10% National Income Share across the world, 2016 (2018, *World Inequality Report,* https://wir2018. wid.world/files/download/wir2018-full-report-english.pdf)

Approximate portions of GNI and GDP by Income Stratum by Daniel Brockman.

Share of growth captured by income groups, 1980-2016 (WID.world 2017, World Inequality Lab, wir2018. wid.world)

Cumulative Growth in Average Incomes (Congressional Budget Office, https://www.cbo.gov/)

18 Encyclopedic Glossary

Noah Webster, ca. 1825 [Samuel-F-B-Morse_Portrait-of-Noah-Webster_circa-1825.jpg] | *Portrait of Noah Webster* by Samuel F. B. Morse, circa 1825 (Wikimedia, https://commons.wikimedia.org/wiki/File:Portrait_of_Noah_Webster.jpg)

The Curve of Laffer (artist's reconstruction, 2020) by Daniel Brockman

Optimal Taxation. Dotted line estimates the Sweet Spot. From Stantcheva and Saez. *A Simpler Theory of Optimal Capital Taxation* (2018, *Journal of Public Economics.* https://emlab.berkeley.edu/~saez/saez-stantchevaJpubE18optKtax.pdf)

Average Tax Rates by Income Groups (two images) from Saez, Zucman, *Progressive Wealth Taxation* (Oct 2019, Brookings Papers on Economic Activity, final draft, emlab.berkeley.edu/~saez/saez-zucmanBPEA19slides.pdf)

Approximate portions of GNI and GDP by Income Stratum by Daniel Brockman.

Bottom 50% national income share from Piketty, Saez and Zucman, (May 2018), *Distributional National Accounts: Methods and Estimates for the United States.* (Quarterly Journal of Economics. NBER Working Paper NO. 22945, Dec 2016, https://eml.berkeley.edu/~saez/PSZ2016Slides.pdf)

US Before Tax Income Shares, from Lansing, Kevin J. and Agnieszka Markewicz, (Oct 17, 2016) *Consequences of Rising Income Inequality.* (FRBSF Economic Letter, Federal Reserve Bank of San Francisco. https://www.frbsf.org/economic-research/publications/economic-letter/2016/october/welfare-consequences-of-income-inequality)

Janissary Recruitment in the Balkans by Ali Amir Beg (ca. 1558). (https://commons.wikimedia.org/w/index.php?curid=22361418)

John D. Rockefeller (ca. 1875). Public Domain. (https://commons.wikimedia.org/wiki/File:John-D-Rockefeller-sen.jpg#/media/File:John-D-Rockefeller-sen.jpg)

Wealth shares of bottom 90% and top 0.1% of families (Jan 18, 2019, Saez & Zucman, letter to Senator Warren, https://emlab.berkeley.edu/~saez/saez-zucman-wealthtax-warren-online.pdf)

The Denmark Staff. (Maersk Lines, 1914), Wikimedia.org (shared with attribution under Creative Commons Attribution-Share Alike 2.0 Generic license, https://commons.wikimedia.org/wiki/File:The_staff_(1914)_(7312784848).jpg)

Albert Parsons (undated photo, Public Domain, published 2020 by Chicago Tribune, http://www.chicagomag.com/city-life/May-2020/The-Battle-of-the-Viaduct-1877/)

Afterword

Cassim in the Cave by Maxfield Parrish (1909). Wikimedia Commons.

Sources

The Fat Kitchen by Pieter van der Heyden apres Pieter Breugel (1563). Metropolitan Museum of Art (metmuseum.org).

"The Fat Kitchen" (1563). Pieter van der Heyden apres Pieter Breugel.

Sources

Akerlof, George A. (1970). *The Market for "Lemons": Quality Uncertainty and the Market Mechanism.* The Quarterly Journal of Economics, 84(3), 488-500. doi:10.2307/1879431. https://doi.org/10.2307/1879431. Described in Ator (2004).

Akerlof, George A. and Robert J. Shiller. (2009). *Animal Spirits* (Princeton University Press, http://amzn.to/2iar4Mz)

Akerlof, George A. and Robert J. Shiller. (2015). *Phishing for Phools: The Economics of Manipulation and Deception* (amazon.com/Phishing-Phools-Economics-Manipulation-Deception/dp/0691168318)

Ator, David. (2004). *Lecture – Private Information, Adverse Selection and Market Failure.* https://dspace.mit.edu/bitstream/handle/1721.1/71009/14-03-fall-2004/contents/lecture-notes/lecture14.pdf

Auten, Gerard and Geoffrey Gee. "Income Mobility in the United States: New Evidence from Income Tax Data" (June 2009, National Tax Journal, https://www.ntanet.org/NTJ/62/2/ntj-v62n02p301-28-income-mobility-united-states.pdf)

Baker, Dean. (2016). *Rigged.* Center for Economic and Policy Research. http://deanbaker.net/images/stories/documents/Rigged.pdf

Baquedano, Felix, Yacob Abrehe Zereyesus, Cheryl Christensen and Constanza Valdez. (Jan 2021). *COVID-19 Working Paper: International Food Security Assessment, 2020-2030: COVID-19 Update and Impacts of Food Insecurity.* Economic Research Service, US Department of Agriculture. https://www.ers.usda.gov/publications/pub-details/?pubid=100275 https://www.ers.usda.gov/topics/international-markets-us-trade/global-food-security/

Baquedano, Felix, Yacob Abrehe Zereyesus, Constanza Valdes and Kayode Ajewole. (Jul 2021). Economic Research Service, US Department of Agriculture. https://www.ers.usda.gov/webdocs/outlooks/101733/gfa-32_summary.pdf?v=3873.2

Berger, David J. (Feb 14, 2017). *In Search of Lost Time: What If Delaware Had Not Adopted Shareholder Primacy?* https://ssrn.com/abstract=2916960 http://dx.doi.org/10.2139/ssrn.2916960 https://www.wsgr.com/a/web/39/berger-1017.pdf

Birch, David L. (1981). *Who creates jobs?* The Public Interest, National Affairs. (https://www.nationalaffairs.com/public_interest/detail/who-creates-jobs)

Blanc, Louis. (1851). Organisation du Travail, as quoted in Wikipedia.org https://en.wikipedia.org/wiki/Louis_Blanc

Blomqvist, Ake. (Jan 1987). *Higher Education and the Markets for Educated Labour in LDCS.* The World Bank. (https://documents1.worldbank.org/curated/en/423021467989473658/pdf.EDT54000Higher0hes0and0implications.pdf)

Bowering, Gerhard (ed.). (2013). *The Princeton Encyclopedia of Islamic Political Thought.* Princeton University Press.

Bricker, Jesse, Sarena Goodman, Kevin B. Moore, Alice Henriques Volz, with assistance from Dalton Ruh. (Sep 28, 2020). *Wealth and Income Concentration in the SCF: 1989–2019.* Board of Governors of the Federal Reserve System. https://www.federalreserve.gov/econres/notes/feds-notes/wealth-and-income-concentration-in-the-scf-20200928.htm

Brinton, Crane. (1965). *The Anatomy of Revolution.* Prentice Hall. https://www.amazon.com/Anatomy-Revolution-Crane-Brinton/dp/0394700449

Brockman, Daniel. (Oct 11, 2016). *Intellectual Property and The King of Denmark's Rule.* https://daniel-brockman.blogspot.com/2016/10/intellectual-property-and-king-of.html

Bureau of Economic Analysis. (2015). *Measuring the Economy.* US Department of Commerce. (https://www.bea.gov/sites/default/files/methodologies/nipa_primer.pdf)

Bureau of Economic Analysis, Department of Commerce. "News Release, Gross Domestic Product" (Dec 21, 2018, Public Domain, https://www.bea.gov/system/files/2018-12/gdp3q18_3rd_1.pdf)

Caruso, Anthony. (Feb 2015). Statistics of US Businesses Employment and Payroll Summary: 2012; Summary Statistics by NAICS Sector and Enterprise Employment Size: 2012; Appendix Table 1. US Census Bureau. https://www.census.gov/content/dam/Census/library/publications/2015/econ/g12-susb.pdf

The Chapel Royal. "Tallis and Byrd - Musicians of Tudor Renaissance" (2017, The Chapel Royal at Hampton Court Palace, England. http://www.chapelroyal.org/tallisbyrd.html)

Chetty, Raj and Nathaniel Hendren. (Feb 10, 2018). *The Impacts of Neighborhoods on the Intergenerational Mobility I: Childhood Exposure Effects.* Quarterly Journal of Economics, Feb 10, 2018. https://doi.org/10.1093/qje/qjy007

Chetty, Raj and Nathaniel Hendren. (Feb 10, 2018). *The Impacts of Neighborhoods on the Intergenerational Mobility II: County-Level Estimates*. Quarterly Journal of Economics, Feb 10, 2018. https://doi.org/10.1093/qje/qjy006

Chetty, Raj, Nathaniel Hendren, Patrick Kline and Emmanuel Saez. (Sep 14, 2014). *Where is the land of Opportunity? The Geography of Intergenerational Mobility in the United States*. Quarterly Journal of Economics, Sep 14, 2014. https://doi.org/10.1093/qje/qju022

Campbell, Joseph in conversation with Michael Toms. (1989). An Open Life. Harper & Row.

Coleman, J.R. (1974). *Blue Collar Journal*. http://amzn.to/2mQus2k

Coleman-Jensen, A., M.P. Rabbitt, C.A. Gregory and A. Singh. (Sep 2016). *Household Food Security in the United States in 2015*. US Department of Agriculture. https://www.ers.usda.gov/webdocs/publications/79761/err-215.pdf?v=42636

Davis, Kenneth C. (2002) *Don't Know Much About History*. https://www.arlingtonschools.org/site/handlers/filedownloadashx?moduleinstanceid=30407&dataid=33099&FileName=Dont_Know_Much_About_History_pdf_BOOK.pdf

Dodge v. Ford Motor Co., 204 Mich. 459, 170 N.W. 668 (Mich. 1919). https://casetext.com/case/dodge-v-ford-motor-co

Drucker, Peter. (2001). *The Essential Drucker*. Harper Business.

East India Company. *Our History*. Retrieved Aug 17, 2021, from https://www.theeastindiacompany.com/about-the-east-india-company-eic/our-history/

East India Company Charter. (1600). https://en.wikisource.org/wiki/Charter_Granted_by_Queen_Elizabeth_to_the_East_India_Company

Engels, Friedrich. (1845). *The Condition of the Working Class in England*. 1886 American Edition, first published 1845, republished by Penguin 1987, https://smile.amazon.com/dp/B099TLJN9W/ref=cm_sw_em_r_mt_dp_DK3JPSHRX23H51N304KF

Engels, Friedrich and Paul Sweezy (tr). (1847). *The Principles of Communism*. Creative Commons Attribution-ShareAlike 2.0 license. https://www.marxists.org/archive/marx/works/1847/11/prin-com.htm

European Commission, et al. (2009). *System of National Accounts 2008*. https://unstats.un.org/unsd/nationalaccount/docs/SNA2008.pdf

Fernandez-Armesto, Felipe. (2007). *Amerigo: The Man Who Gave His Name to America*. Random House. http://a.co/cl3Q6mw

Farley, Robert. "Dependency and Romney's 47 Percenters" (Sep 2012, FactCheck.org, https://www.factcheck.org/2012/09/dependency-and-romneys-47-percenters/)

Frankopan, Peter. (2015). *The Silk Roads: A New History of the World*. Bloomsbury, Knopf, Vintage.

Gerdeman, D. (Oct 3, 2016). Clayton Christensen: The Theory of Jobs To Be Done. Working Knowledge: Business Research for Business Leaders, Harvard Business School. http://hbswk.hbs.edu/item/clay-christensen-the-theory-of-jobs-to-be-done

Goldstein, Jacob and Lam Thuy Vo. "The 47 Percent, In One Graphic" (Sep 2012, National Public Radio, https://www.npr.org/sections/money/2012/09/18/161337343/the-47-percent-in-one-graphic)

Greene, Richard. (1982). *Tracking job growth in private industry*. Monthly Labor Review, Bureau of Labor Statistics, US Dept. of Labor. (https://www.bls.gov/opub/mlr/1982/09/art1full.pdf)

Greenspan, Alan. (Feb 27, 2004). *Intellectual property rights*. The Federal Reserve Board. https://www.federalreserve.gov/boarddocs/speeches/2004/200402272/

Haslam, Bill quoted in Wermund (Jan 16, 2019).

Hessenland, F. *The Sound Dues of Denmark, and their Relations with the Commerce of the World*. Translated in Hunt's Merchant's Magazine (Oct 1855). Reprinted with related statements by the President of the United States in *The North American Review*. (Jan 1857). Vol. 84, No. 174, pp. 48-70. https://www.jstor.org/stable/25104806?seq=2#metadata_info_tab_contents

Hill, Andrew. (Jun 12, 2013). *The management revolution*. Financial Times. https://www.ft.com/content/25def0a6-d352-11e2-b3ff-00144feab7de

Hughes, I. (1977). *New Guinea Stone Age Trade*. Dept. of Prehistory, Australian National University. https://pacificinstitute.anu.edu.au/sites/default/files/resources-links/TA_03.pdf

Internal Revenue Service. (2018 tax year). Table 1.1. All Returns: Selected Income and Tax Items (18in11si.xls). https://www.irs.gov/statistics/soi-tax-stats-individual-statistical-tables-by-size-of-adjusted-gross-income

Internal Revenue Service. (2001-2017 tax years). Table 1. All Individual Returns Excluding Dependents (17in01etr.xls). https://www.irs.gov/statistics/soi-tax-stats-individual-statistical-tables-by-tax-rate-and-income-percentile#earlyRelease

IRS. See Internal Revenue Service.

Joy, Bill. (Apr 2000). *Why the Future Doesn't Need Us*. Wired, Conde Nast. https://www.wired.com/2000/04/joy-2/

Kearney, Joseph D. (Jan 1, 1999). *From the Fall of the Bell System to the Telecommunications Act: Regulation of Telecommunications Under Judge Greene*. Marquette Law Scholarly Commons, Marquette University Law School. http://scholarship.law.marquette.edu/cgi/viewcontent.cgi?article=1503&context=facpub

Kelly, Marjorie. (2001, 2003). *The Divine Right of Capital*. Berrett-Koehler Publishers.

Kiel, Paul. (Nov 14, 2008). *AIG's Spiral Downward: A Timeline*. ProPublica.

Kindleberger, Charles P. (1978). *Manias, Panics and Crashes*. Basic Books.

Kitson, P.M., Leigh Shaw-Taylor, E.A. Wrigley, R.S. Davies, G. Newton, and M. Satchell (May 2010). *The creation of a 'census' of adult male employment for England and Wales for 1817*. Cambridge Group for the History of Population and Social Structure, Department of Geography, University of Cambridge. http://www.geog.cam.ac.uk/research/projects/occupations/britain19c/papers/paper2.pdf

Krugman, Paul. (Feb 16, 2021). Arguing With Zombies. (Norton).

Krugman, Paul. (Jun 20, 2013). "Profits Without Production" (New York Times, http://www.nytimes.com/2013/06/21/opinion/krugman-profits-without-production.html)

Lansing, Kevin and Agnieszka Markiewicz. (Oct 17, 2016). *Consequences of Rising Income Inequality*. FRBSF Economic Letter. Federal Reserve Bank of San Francisco. http://www.frbsf.org/economic-research/publications/economic-letter/2016/october/welfare-consequences-of-income-inequality/

The Learning Network. *(May 15, 2012). May 15, 1911 | Supreme Court Orders Standard Oil to Be Broken Up.* New York Times. https://learning.blogs.nytimes.com/2012/05/15/may-15-1911-supreme-court-orders-standard-oil-to-be-broken-up

Lewis, Robert (Aug 9, 2007) quoted in United States District Court, Southern District of New York. *In Re American International Group, Inc, 2008 Securities Litigation.* Master File No.: 08-CV-4772-LTS. (See also Kiel [Nov 14, 2008]) https://barrack.com/sites/default/files/AIG%20Lead%20Plaintiff's%20Memo%20of%20Law%20in%20Opp%20to%20Motions%20to%20Dismiss.pdf

Lubin, Gus. (Jul 16, 2013). *Everyone Needs To Stop Hating On That Sample Budget From McDonald's.* Business Insider. https://www.businessinsider.com/mcdonalds-sample-budget-is-actually-fine-2013-7

Marx, Karl, Friedrich Engels, Samuel Moore (tr) and Dr. Aveling (tr). (1867). *Capital: A Critique of Political Economy* (a.k.a. *Das Kapital*). Digireads.com Publishing (ebook 2010). http://amzn.to/2jmOjac

Marx, Karl, Friedrich Engels and Samuel Moore (tr). (1848). *Manifesto of the Communist Party,* (English translation, 1888). 1908 New York Labor News Edition. http://amzn.to/2hl0LCS and Marx/Engels Internet Archive. Creative Commons Attribution-ShareAlike license. https://www.marxists.org/archive/marx/works/1848/communist-manifesto/index.htm

Massie, R.K. (1980). Peter the Great. http://amzn.to/2nu5GTU

Moorhead, Molly. "Mitt Romney says 47 percent of Americans pay no income tax" (Sep 2012, Politifact, http://www.politifact.com/truth-o-meter/statements/2012/sep/18/mitt-romney/romney-says-47-percent-americans-pay-no-income-tax/)

Murphy, Ed. We regret we have mislaid our note citing the source of our information regarding Professor "Captain" Ed Murphy.

Nasdaq, Inc. (Jul 27, 2013). *McDonald's Sample Budget Sheet Is Laughable, but Its Implications Are Not.* https://www.nasdaq.com/articles/mcdonalds-sample-budget-sheet-laughable-its-implications-are-not-2013-07-27

Piketty, Thomas. Tr. Arthur Goldhammer. (2020). Capital and Ideology. https://www.amazon.com/dp/0674980824

Piketty, Thomas. Tr. Arthur Goldhammer. (2014). Capital in the Twenty-First Century. Belknap Harvard. https://www.amazon.com/dp/0674979850

Piketty, Thomas, Emmanuel Saez, Gabriel Zucman. "Distributional National Accounts: Methods and Estimates for the United States" (May 2018, Quarterly Journal of Economics, https://eml.berkeley.edu/~saez/PSZ2018QJE.pdf)

Piketty, Thomas, Emmanuel Saez and Stefanie Stantcheva. (2014). *Optimal Taxation of Top Labor Incomes: A Tale of Three Elasticities.* https://eml.berkeley.edu/~saez/piketty-saez-stantchevaAEJ14.pdf

Rand, Ayn. (1957). *Atlas Shrugged.* Penguin.

Rand, Ayn. (1961). *The Virtue of Selfishness.* Penguin.

Ricardo, David. (1821). *On the Principles of Political Economy and Taxation.* (http://www.econlib.org/library/Ricardo/ricP.html)

Ritter, Joseph A. (Dec 1993). *Measuring Labor Market Dynamics: Gross Flows of Workers and Jobs.* Review, Economic Research, Federal Reserve Bank of St. Louis. (https://files.stlouisfed.org/files/htdocs/publications/review/93/11/Labor_Nov_Dec1993.pdf)

Roberts, John. Quoted in Rubenstein (2019).

Rubenstein, David M. (2019). *The American Story.* Simon & Schuster.

Saez, Emmanuel and Gabriel Zucman. (Oct 2020). *Trends in US Income and Wealth Inequality: Revising after the Revisionists.* Working Paper 27921, National Bureau of Economic Research. (https://www.nber.org/papers/w27921 https://eml.berkeley.edu/~saez/SaezZucman2020NBER.pdf)

Saez, Emmanuel. (Feb 2020). *Striking it Richer: The Evolution of Top Incomes in the United States.* UC Berkeley. https://emlab.berkeley.edu/~saez/saez-UStopincomes-2018.pdf

Saez, Emmanuel. (Jun 30, 2016). *Striking it Richer.* http://eml.berkeley.edu/~saez/saez-UStopincomes-2015.pdf.

Saez, Emmanuel and Gabriel Zucman. (May 2016). *Wealth Inequality in the United States since 1913.* The Quarterly Journal of Economics. http://eml.berkeley.edu/~saez/SaezZucman2016QJE.pdf, http://eml.berkeley.edu/~saez/SaezZucman2016QJEAppendix.pdf.

Santelli, Rick. (Feb 19, 2009). *We're thinking of having a Chicago Tea Party in July.* CNBC video. https://youtu.be/zp-Jw-5Kx8k?t=125. For Santelli's full statement: https://youtu.be/zp-Jw-5Kx8k

Schwartz, Pedro. (Nov 7, 2016). *Capitalism and Its Names.* Library of Economics and Liberty. http://www.econlib.org/library/Columns/y2016/Schwartzcapitalism.html

Semega, Jessica, Melissa Kollar, John Creamer and Abinash Mohanty. (Sep 10, 2019). *Income and Poverty in the United States: 2018.* United States Census Bureau, https://www.census.gov/content/dam/Census/library/publications/2019/demo/p60-266.pdf

Seth, Shobhit. (Mar 10, 2019) *GDP vs. GNP: What's the Difference?* Investopedia, https://www.investopedia.com/ask/answers/030415/what-functional-difference-between-gdp-and-gnp.asp

Shin, Laura. "Why McDonald's Employee Budget Has Everyone Up In Arms" (Jul 18, 2013, Forbes, https://www.forbes.com/sites/laurashin/2013/07/18/why-mcdonalds-employee-budget-has-everyone-up-in-arms/#5e592aa15216)

Sismondi, J.C.L. Simonde de. Biography.com. https://www.biography.com/people/jcl-simonde-de-sismondi-37535

Smith, Adam. (1776). *An Inquiry into the Nature and Causes of the Wealth of Nations.* http://amzn.to/2jjusby

Smith, Adam. (1759). *The Theory of Moral Sentiments.* 2010 republication by Digireads, http://amzn.to/2ADCAYL

Smith, Michael D. and Birgit Meade. (2019). Who Are the World's Food Insecure? US Department of Agriculture, Economic Research Service. https://www.ers.usda.gov/amber-waves/2019/june/who-are-the-world-s-food-insecure-identifying-the-risk-factors-of-food-insecurity-around-the-world/

Snepscheut, Jan L. A. van de. (retrieved Apr 2017). On Theory and Practice. Wikiquote https://en.wikiquote.org/wiki/Jan_L._A._van_de_Snepscheut

Stiglitz, Joseph E. (Dec 8, 2001). "Information and the Change in the Paradigm in Economics" (Prize Lecture, https://www.nobelprize.org/nobel_prizes/economic-sciences/laureates/2001/stiglitz-lecture.pdf)

Stiglitz, Joseph E. (Apr 8, 2013). "The Price of Inequality: How Today's Divided Society Endangers Our Future" (amazon.com/Price-Inequality-Divided-Society-Endangers/dp/0393345068)

Tuchman, Barbara. (1978). *A Distant Mirror*. Random House.

US Census Bureau. *U.S. and World Population Clock.* https://www.census.gov/popclock/world

US Census Bureau. "Income and Poverty in the United States: 2016." Table A-2 (https://www.census.gov/library/publications/2017/demo/p60-259.html, https://www2.census.gov/programs-surveys/demo/tables/p60/259/tableA2.xls)

US Census Bureau. "Number in Poverty and Poverty Rate: 1959 to 2016" (1960 to 2017, Current Population Survey, https://census.gov/content/dam/Census/library/visualizations/2017/demo/p60-259/figure4.pdf)

US Census Bureau. "Poverty Thresholds" (2016, https://www2.census.gov/programs-surveys/cps/tables/time-series/historical-poverty-thresholds/thresh16.xls)

US Department of Agriculture, Economic Research Service. "Key Statistics & Graphics, Food Security Status of U.S. Households in 2016" (https://www.ers.usda.gov/topics/food-nutrition-assistance/food-security-in-the-us/key-statistics-graphics.aspx)

US Department of Agriculture, Economic Research Service. "Key Statistics & Graphics" (retrieved Mar 27, 2018, https://www.ers.usda.gov/topics/food-nutrition-assistance/food-security-in-the-us/key-statistics-graphics.aspx)

US Department of Agriculture, Economic Research Service. "Poverty, Percent of total population in poverty, 2016" (retrieved Jun 11, 2018, https://data.ers.usda.gov/reports.aspx?ID=17826)

US Department of Health & Human Services, "U.S. Federal Poverty Guidelines Used to Determine Financial Eligibility for Certain Federal Programs" (retrieved Jun 11, 2018, https://aspe.hhs.gov/poverty-guidelines)

Veblen, Thorsten. (1899). *The Theory of the Leisure Class*. Oxford University Press, Oxford World's Classics Kindle edition (2007). Originally published by Macmillan.

Weissmann, Jordan. (Jul 16, 2013). *McDonald's Can't Figure Out How Its Workers Survive on Minimum Wage*. https://www.theatlantic.com/business/archive/2013/07/mcdonalds-cant-figure-out-how-its-workers-survive-on-minimum-wage/277845/

Wermund, Benjamin. (Jan 16, 2019). *The red state that loves free college*. (Politico, https://www.politico.com/agenda/story/2019/01/16/tennessee-free-college-000867, retrieved Mar 1, 2019)

Wikipedia. *Sound Dues*. https://en.wikipedia.org/wiki/Sound_Dues

Wikiquote. "A man always has two reasons...". Quote attributed to J.P. Morgan by Owen Wister in 1930. https://en.wikiquote.org/wiki/Reason

Wilmeth, R. (1973). *Distribution of Several Types of Obsidian From Archaeological Sites in British Columbia* (esp. comments by Stryd, A. H. and P. Donahue). Bulletin, Canadian Archaeological Association. https://www.jstor.org/stable/41243012

The World Bank. GDP & GNI data series (retrieved Jan 28, 2019, https://databank.worldbank.org/data/reports.aspx?source=2&series=NY.GNS.ICTR.ZS#)

World Inequality Lab. (2017) *World Inequality Report 2018*. (Non-commercial use by CC license https://creativecommons.org/licenses/by-nc-sa/4.0/, https://wir2018.wid.world/files/download/wir2018-full-report-english.pdf)

Younkins, Edward W. (2002). *Capitalism and Commerce*. Lexington Books. https://smile.amazon.com/dp/0739103806/

Zweig, Jason. (2015). *Devil's Financial Dictionary*. PublicAffairs. https://smile.amazon.com/Devils-Financial-Dictionary-Jason-Zweig/dp/1610397762/

Zweig, Jason. (Nov 13, 2021). *GE and the Belief in Management Magic*. Wall Street Journal. https://www.wsj.com/articles/ge-what-went-wrong-11636762439

About the Author

Daniel Brockman

Dan has Mathematics and Finance degrees and lifelong interest in history and economics. He worked in statistical analysis and software development in investment companies and banks for 30 years. Dan swims, hikes, and rides his bicycle near his home in the state of Washington, USA.

Interested in reading more?

https://www.laughingphilosopher.com

www.ingramcontent.com/pod-product-compliance
Lightning Source LLC
Chambersburg PA
CBHW050349230426
43663CB00010B/2046